TEACHERS OF MYTH

TEACHERS OF MYTH

*Interviews on Educational and Psychological
Uses of Myth with Adolescents*

Maren Tonder Hansen

Spring Journal Books
New Orleans, Louisiana

Published by
Spring Journal, Inc.
627 Ursulines Street #7
New Orleans, Louisiana 70116
Tel.: (504) 524-5117
Fax: (504) 558-0088
Website: www.springjournalandbooks.com

Printed in Canada.
Text printed on acidfree paper.

Cover Art, "The Mermaid"
by John William Waterhouse
used by permission
Royal Academy of Arts, London

Cover design by
Northern Cartographic
4050 Williston Road
South Burlington, Vermont 05403

Library in Congress Cataloging in Publication Data
Pending

DEDICATION

I dedicate this book to my beloved mother,
Lois Ann Snyder Hansen,
a high school teacher of English and psychology,
who taught me in ways that continue to unfold.

ACKNOWLEDGMENTS

I want to acknowledge the ways that Joseph Campbell shaped my relationship to myth. He eloquently told the world's great stories, often simultaneously illustrated by slides. When he spoke I could feel that the myth was personal to him, that he had taken the collective wisdom inside himself, letting it befriend and mentor him. Through this integration into his own being, he led me into the ongoing dialogue between the great collective stories and the inner meaning of an individual's life. Campbell had a living relationship with myth. We could feel the meaning of the myth through him. I was deeply touched by him as a person and a teacher.

I am grateful to my husband, Stephen Aizenstat, for love, encouragement, and believing in my work. Our children, Jesse, Alia, and Eli have generously provided field research in adolescent psychological development. My intimacy with each of them has vivified the lived meanings of myth.

I thank my editor and publisher Nancy Cater, of Spring Journal Books, for her enthusiasm about these interviews and her can-do professional approach. I breathlessly tried to keep pace with her turnaround time, in early morning hours responding to her middle of the night e-mails. The lighthearted fun Nancy brings to the publishing process was a pleasure.

Contents

Introduction

Resurgent interest in the educational and psychological uses of myth is evident among school teachers, youth group leaders, and outdoor educational guides, who are integrating myth into their programs in experimental and creative ways. Yet, most are doing these activities in isolation. We lack appropriate resources, research, or even networking to guide this important work. Basic questions need to be addressed: What do we hope to achieve in teaching myth to youth? What is the relationship between myth and human psychological development? How is it that myth seems to meet people in such a deep way? And finally, what teaching methods help people connect myth to their own lives?

This book contains in-depth interviews with three master teachers of myth, opening a treasure chest of pedagogical wisdom. These gifted teachers articulate theoretical underpinnings and share practical, imaginative methods for teaching myth to adolescents. All have within themselves a rich, living relationship with myth and an intuitive understanding of its psychological dimensions.

The first interview is with Michael Meade. In his work with youth, Meade pounds rhythms on his drum while telling spellbinding stories. He has street smarts as well as book smarts, a commitment to psychological learning, and a humble sense of his own humanity. The second interview is with Betty Staley, who is steeped in the traditions of Rudolf Steiner and the Waldorf Schools. Staley is a seasoned teacher who weaves myth into her high school curricula, consciously holding the relationship between the story and human developmental stages. Staley teaches myth to adolescents and trains other Waldorf teachers in this work. The third interview is with Kent Ferguson. He has co-founded and been headmaster of two innovative schools that integrate myth with academics and a rigorous outdoor education program. Ferguson has been known to lead an entire middle school on bicycles from Southern California to the Four Corners in order that the Navajo myths could be heard around a campfire in their indigenous landscape. Hero's journeys abound!

Why do we care about teaching myth? Perhaps we care because for thousands of years myths have taught us what it means to be human. Myths not only entertain us with fascinating stories, but also offer us companions and mentors for the journey of the human soul. Mysteriously, stories told and retold in lands halfway around the globe two thousand years ago touch our most intimate existential yearnings and struggles. The narratives of myth contain the depth matrix of the psyche, revealing fundamental existential patterns of being human.

I felt honored to participate in these interviews. Sitting with each teacher, I noticed moments when something in the air changed, became dreamlike, and we were suddenly in the magical place of myth. Because myth is grounded in the oral tradition, and I so loved the spoken quality of these dialogues, I chose to edit them lightly. Each interviewee agreed that we would accept literary imperfection in order to allow for the natural feel of conversation.

As a myth is told and retold, so our pedagogy of myth evolves through dialogues. It is my pleasure to offer these interviews into the field. I thank Michael Meade, Betty Staley, and Kent Ferguson for their years of original work in teaching myth, for speaking authentically, and sharing so generously.

Maren Tonder Hansen

CHAPTER ONE

Interview with
Michael Meade

Michael Meade has studied myth, anthropology, history of religion, and cross-cultural rituals for over 35 years. He synthesizes these disciplines, tapping into ancestral sources of wisdom, elucidating enlivened, relevant connections to the stories we are living today. A storyteller *par excellence*, he uses drumming, singing, and rituals to create soulful renditions of ancient myths. In his extensive work with adolescents, Meade evokes the traditions of mentoring and initiation.

Michael Meade

Meade is the author of *Men and the Water of Life*; co-editor, with James Hillman and Robert Bly, of *Rag and Bone Shop of the Heart*; and co-editor of *Crossroads: A Quest for Contemporary Rites of Passage*. He is also the Founder/Director of Mosaic Multicultural Foundation, a network of artists, teachers, and activists that fosters community healing and development efforts.

MAREN HANSEN: In teaching myth to adolescents, what do you hope to achieve?

MICHAEL MEADE: There are two things that I'm usually thinking of beforehand. First of all, I hope their imagination gets caught, and they have an experience of what I call mythological thinking or symbolic thinking, an opening of the psyche wherein they realize that an image has become a symbol for them. They suddenly see something symbolically; that's the "aha," the mythical awakening to the world of meaning, which I think most young people are seeking.

Then the second part is that I hope they connect to something symbolic and meaningful in themselves. I hope they get a sense that they are part of a big story. That they are carrying a story, and that if they live that story out, they will somehow be connected to the culture and to the cosmos. So, I'm looking for "oh, wow, I get it!", and then to have that become personal.

HANSEN: So, in your work it's important to you that adolescents not only understand the myth, but also bring it inside.

MEADE: Yes. Usually I'm telling them stories, assuming that myth has two basic meanings: learning the symbolic aspects of the story and the actual telling of the story. I make every effort to make sure that the kids wind up *in* the story and find their own story through that.

HANSEN: How do you help them find themselves in the story?

MEADE: I tell stories usually while drumming, you know that. So really what's going on is a light form of trance. I'm doing a very light induction through certain kind of rhythms and speech. That pulls their consciousness into the story. Then I have the simplest technique I've ever found. I say, "What struck you in the story?" I wait. I try to give everyone a chance to speak. Naturally, some are reluctant and some will go very quickly. I'll try to get them all speaking, unless the group is really large. Then, I can show them that everybody has a slightly different view, even if it's the same spot in the story, each is seeing it differently. Once we're there, I can say, "the different way in which you see is your view of the world. If you pay attention to that, you start to realize where you are in the great drama of life." I find that's the most valuable thing to communicate directly to young people.

Recently, I was at an alternative school with about three hundred students. I worked with the whole group all day long. Afterwards, I received a big envelope. Many of them wrote notes: "I'm the one who said this." "I'm the one who said that." "I hope you remember me, I said this." That's what I'm after. The recognition of the uniqueness of "I." The fact that "I" spoke. The teachers at the lunch break were saying, "Did you see who spoke up?" It was the kids who don't usually talk in class. "I said this" tells me they were symbolically connected because they can reference points in the story connected to their lives. They know that I'm trying to see them. They understand. They want to be seen having a deep connection to the story of life. Most kids are smart enough to know that what they say is really about them. I seek out stories that tend to provoke personal reactions.

HANSEN: What stories have you noticed adolescents tend to find themselves in?

MEADE: Initiatory stories. Stories that have a pretty clear initiatory path. Stories that have a girl or a boy struggling in it, a prince or a princess. I like village tales because everyone can identify with them.

HANSEN: Village tales?

MEADE: Folk tales, or folk myths. There's often a point in the story where someone has to leave the village. So after I've told the story I say, "What struck you?"

Inevitably someone will say, "Well, he had to leave the village and he was all by himself."

Then I'll say, "So, is that where you are now in your life?"

And he'll say, "Well, I'm not by myself because I've got my friends, but yeah. Yeah."

And I say, "That's what happens at your age. You're with your friends, and you're all alone. You're alone in order to reveal yourself to yourself." I talk to them straight out like that.

And they say, "What do you mean?"

And I say, "Well, everybody wants you to be this way or that way, but something inside you wants you to be you, and that's what's happening now." They get it quickly. So, I hunt for stories that open that territory.

Some stories have an explicit ordeal. The best story I've ever found for working with kids is the story of the Half-boy. As a half-person he leaves the village and meets another half. Instead of joining together they have a big fight, and they fall into a river. They disappear into the river. Sometimes I'll stop the story and ask, "What's the river?" Someone will say alcohol. Someone will say drugs. Someone will say depression. The kids will name their own symptoms and struggles. The river becomes a symbol that each one relates to.

If you're not paying attention, you're missing a big opportunity, because the kids will tell you what they're dealing with. Violence. Abuse. They'll just say it out loud, in front of everybody.

Actually, to refine the point a bit, when they find a symbolic reference point, young people usually will indicate the way in which they're gifted and the way in which they're wounded. They'll do it so quickly that it amazes me, even though I've seen it a thousand times. Some will start with the wounded place, while others start out with the gifted place. Secretly, the two places are related. It's kind of a self-revelation that I think is natural; young people are looking to reveal things. I think some of the disappointment that you find in young people is because this appointment that they expected to have with their inner Self, this revelation of the Self, hasn't happened. So, they're dis-appointed because they haven't found the biologically, psychologically, mythologically expected appointment.

HANSEN: I'm not fully understanding what you're saying. Did you say, "dis-appointed?"

MEADE: I'm playing with the words. They expected an appointment with their genuine inner self. In certain cultures they call the initiation or rites of passage a self-revelation. What's revealed is the symbolic core of the Self. Everybody expects it. It's a biological, psychological, mythological expectation. When it doesn't happen, there is an increasing sense of disorientation and disappointment.

I thought high school was going to be the thing that I was waiting for. I expected a 'higher' school. I was incredibly disappointed. I told the teachers, "I didn't come here for this. I thought we were going to deal with real things." They said, "What do you mean? We've got history, we've got math." I said, "But I thought we were going to really do it." They didn't know what I was talking about.

HANSEN: You thought the teachers would do that?

MEADE: Oh, yeah.

HANSEN: Had that happened for you in previous school years?

MEADE: Well, it happened to me on my thirteenth birthday when my aunt accidentally gave me Edith Hamilton's *Greek Myths*. She didn't know what it was about or what it would mean to me.

HANSEN: How did she accidentally give it to you?

MEADE: I was interested in history at the time, and I think I told her something about mythology. I can't remember. After she gave the book to me, she said, "I hope that's all right. I wasn't even sure that was the book I meant to get." It was one of those beautiful accidents.

I read most of it that night and realized, "Oh, wow, this is what I'm looking for." That was the year I started high school. I remember even saying to the history teacher, "Are you going to get to the older history, mythology?" He said, "No, this is history." I understood it as a dis-appointment. It was only later on that I started to think, *well maybe I was dis-appointed because I expected a real appointment, like a meeting where you are appointed to be yourself.* Now that I work with a lot of youth, I try not to miss such moments.

HANSEN: The appointments?

MEADE: If a young person is trying to show me a genuine aspect of herself or himself, I will say something directly to them even at the risk of being wrong or offending.

HANSEN: Will you reflect back to them what you see?

MEADE: Yes, and I'll do it right in front of everybody. A young person risks speaking out, and I'll say, "Well, you have kind of a philosophical gene there; that's a very philosophical take on that issue."

And she'll say, "What?"

And I'll say, "Well, I think you have a philosophical tendency, which is a really great thing." And I say, "You probably already know that." And she'll kind of nod her head.

That person will usually come up afterwards and say, "What does that mean—to be philosophical?"

And I'll say, "Well, *philo-sophia*, it means that you love knowledge. That's a wonderful thing to know, because you may pursue that your whole life, or just part of your life." I just try to give kids the idea that they have something already coming out of them, and I can see them trying to reach their appointed pathway.

HANSEN: I'm struck with how hungry adolescents are to be seen.

MEADE: Jesus. *(pause)* Yep. And inside they know it. That's why the comments they wrote to me were so interesting: "I'm the one that said..." They were hoping to be seen.

I also talk to them honestly. I'll tell them right at the beginning, "You know, you're living through a hard time. What you're going through is more difficult than when I was your age." There are certain ways in which that's true, and I'll tell them that. I say, "Some things are much harder now, and you're going to live through it." That helps them to realize, *well, maybe its okay to name what I'm struggling with.* They are trying to have an authentic experience of life. So I try to meet them there if I can. But I also know that the story does it automatically. Stories invite the whole awareness of the listeners.

HANSEN: Let's explore that. I'm hearing how you function psychologically with the kids. You are seeing them, you are telling them who you see, you're validating their struggles in their lives. Can you talk about the relationship between the mythic story that you use and your psychological working of it? That's a big ball field, but let's expand into that.

MEADE: Well, this is a bit of a crude comparison, but to me the story functions like an x-ray. I tell stories over and over. For me, the story becomes a field or a territory. The territory gets established between the teller, the listeners, and me. So if someone says, "Well, what intrigued me is how when the half-boy comes out of the river he's disoriented," automatically I see them in the story at that spot. I visually, imaginally see them against that specific symbolic scenery. From knowing the story, and having heard a lot of people speak into it and having worked on it myself, I know that they have placed themselves where the youth is both whole for the first time and disoriented in the world.

I'm figuring, well, most young people are disoriented so that's no surprise. But, I'm calculating kind of quickly, how disoriented do they look, what words are they using? I'm trying to see their exact issue. Sometimes there's actually a critical problem. On occasion, I will go to the teachers afterward and say, "Great class, and by the way, this kid's in trouble in a way that may not be obvious." The story becomes like an x-ray. When you learn the territory of the story, then each area has mythic and psychological value. As soon as a person identifies "I'm here in the story," it's as if they told me a dream of theirs; they have revealed the shape of their inner life. I see it that way. I become alert to the words they're using, also. Just like doing dream interpretation.

HANSEN: Yes. It's very much like working with a dream, or at least how I work with a dream.

MEADE: They're very similar. You could even say I have laid out a dream and they've walked into it. And then I'm saying, "Look where you are in the dream, let's amplify that." It all happens very fast. I try to just be open to it and go with what appears.

HANSEN: So you're always thinking metaphorically, in the interactions, as well as in the myth. Do you think that part of how you convey the psychological meaning of the myth is through your metaphoric thinking and speaking?

MEADE: Yes, I use metaphorical language throughout. And I'll adjust as we go along, because there will be a group metaphor, almost invariably, a collective metaphor appears. I will try to elucidate that and name it. I might use poems, or I might spontaneously connect the group metaphor to another story to elaborate it. What I'm continually doing is inviting them into the mythic, metaphorical land.

HANSEN: Are there kids who don't understand it?

7

MEADE: Basically, I would say no. Now, there are kids who don't get it the way others get it. I remember one kid in Chicago said, "This is impossible what you're saying, don't you see that it's impossible?" He meant illogical, and he kept going emphatically on that. I realized he was having a mental problem; he was banging his head against something. He couldn't shift to metaphorical thought. Afterwards, there was a debriefing with the teachers. I asked, "Has he had any kind of mental problems?" And they said, "Well, we've been wondering." And I said, "Well, I would try to have that checked out." He was trying so hard to be present, to be metaphorical, and he couldn't get there. That could be a sign of abuse or some other serious problem.

HANSEN: The ability to think symbolically—if you subscribe to Piaget's cognitive stages—really starts developing at the onset of adolescence. Your approach to myth centers on metaphoric, symbolic thinking, which is perfect for adolescents and adults. I wonder whether you ever work with younger kids, younger than teens, because I imagine it would require a different approach.

MEADE: I do, but I prefer to work with teens and older. Often I'll do community events. I was doing something recently and there were children, infants in arms, and all the way up to eighty-year-old people—the whole range. That's fine. There are things I like about that. The children walk up to me while I'm telling stories and walk around. I like that. They're not into sitting down. They like wandering through the story, between the story and the audience.

But I'm particularly interested in how the psyche opens up in what we call adolescence or youth. I've made a decades-long study of initiatory experiences, and I think they're critical to understanding youth. To me, the inevitable wounding of childhood has its best chance of being healed in adolescence because the psyche opens so wide and becomes so fluid. You look at that painting [a painting of a young child that we had seen earlier], and you can't tell if it's a girl or a boy because it doesn't know if it's a girl or a boy for a while. It becomes that fluid. During childhood the ego develops as the agent of the psyche or soul in relation to the outer world. The ego or persona is the aspect of the psyche related to the specifics of time and place; it must deal with the 'real world' and its limitations. At the end of the road of childhood, each young person enters a crossroads in which the inner life becomes intensified and ready for change. In the story of the Half-boy, the river represents the fluid state in which the child struggles and sinks and swims to reach the other side of childhood. In order to become conscious of one's genuine purpose in this life, the psyche must become fluid and open to radical change.

In that fluidity a tremendous amount of healing can occur. I think that the culture misunderstands that and backs away from young people right at the point where they could be most healed, reshaped, and reoriented. Adolescents are capable of rapid growth. They're capable of deep understanding and healing. So I approach them that way. I approach my work as "Today's the day we're going to have self-revelatory experiences." *(laughter)* Me too. Because I feel the place of radical change remains open throughout life.

HANSEN: What kind of psychological growth do you hope for in the adolescents you work with?

MEADE: Often, I only see young people once. I come in as a traveling storyteller. So, I'm looking for the opening experience. I'm looking for— *(looks around room and eyes land on a crucifix)* I think I'm being affected by this place *(he grins)*—a confirmation.

HANSEN: You're being affected by this place? Is that what you're saying? *(The interview is taking place in a Catholic retreat center.) (laughter)*

MEADE: Yeah, it's affecting my language. Confirmation is a Christian remnant of a rite of passage. The ambience suggests that word.

HANSEN: Okay. Let's just watch that.

MEADE: I've had so many teachers say, "I really want to thank you for being here today and seeing so-and-so and confirming them." They say, "That kid has been lost. That girl, she hardly ever speaks. We're amazed that she spoke. The way you held her attention and gave her some confirmation is just… really a great thing."

HANSEN: You hope there's an opening so the kids feel confirmed and— what? That the world's a larger place than they had thought?

9

MEADE: Yes. And that they're a part of it in an essential way. They must be genuinely seen and in a specific, memorable context. I'll say to kids, "That's a really good way of saying that. Could you repeat it again so everybody can hear it?" Or I'll repeat it. "Did you hear what she just said? Now, that's a smart thing to say, and here's why." Sometimes I'll load in some—what would you call that—educational stuff. "Here's why I know she said a smart thing. Here's what's implied in what she just said." And so in a sense I'm making her the teacher of the group by proxy, and it works.

One of the things I remember about being young is being talked down to. I didn't like it. It seems to me that by around twelve or thirteen, fourteen for sure, girls and boys are having serious ideas. They're having their core seed ideas. I like the old perspective, which is that you're born seeded with ideas. I figure part of the job of anybody working with kids in the mythic arena is to water those seeds, to get some of the water of abundance onto their seeds. I try to find ways to do that. I've noticed that they're not only hungry, they're readily grateful, and oftentimes it's the kids in trouble who will respond most quickly. So, that's another benefit. Kids who are in trouble will often get the metaphors because they're forced into a part of the psyche that's struggling to understand beyond the obvious. Teachers are often surprised. They say, "You know, some of these kids are really smart. But it seems to be the other kids who most understand what you are doing." I say, "Yes, for a change." I think it's an extremely dynamic opportunity to be present at a unique intersection. I call it living myth or living symbolism.

HANSEN: When you have opportunities to work with myths more deeply over time with a group of kids, what kind of psychological development do you think could happen, or does happen?

MEADE: I think that young people can't help but reveal their psychological shape. I don't make a diagnosis or anything, but I try to grasp the shape that they're offering. Working repeatedly with kids, I'll notice that with a certain boy, in every story that's told, he's intrigued with, or attracted to, or repulsed by, the conflict part of it. That's what compels him. So then I think, this is the shape of his psyche, at least for now. This is one who's attracted to the conflict. Whereas, you'll see someone else who's very, very different. And then, I try to underscore that. *(The light in the room dims.)*

HANSEN: That's a confirmation.

MEADE: *(laughter)* I also try to offer them some psychological terms. Not necessarily diagnostic terms, but language that carries psyche. Engage them in psychological conversation and give clear permission that psychological awareness and learning is part of what we're all here to do together. Perhaps there will be a problem or a disagreement, and someone will say "Oh, that's ridiculous." And I'll say, "Well, wait a minute, it might be ridiculous from where you're sitting, and we'll come to that, but let's look at why it has value, why someone could see things that way. It might be ridiculous to you because you're seeing things so differently, but let's look at that." I try to catch them in their psychological postures and hold them there to deepen it. And they'll do it.

HANSEN: Is this really a form of group psychotherapy?

MEADE: Well, part of it is, because psychology is how people get to mythology now. *(pause)* I think. Mostly, Western culture is psychologized. Currently, psychology is the bridge to myth. If I can get kids doing some psychological thinking or feeling, then it's easier to get to the mythic part of it. Psychology is an easier ground. They're kind of used to it.

I remember James Hillman saying that all real learning is psychological. Well, myths have a level of psychology automatically, so it's one place to engage. But also I think it's helpful to get the sense across to young people that learning has a psychological level, that they should be learning psychologically because it will help them understand issues at school and issues in their family. Stories seem to invite psychological learning. I guess it's psychotherapeutic. Kind of sudden therapy.

HANSEN: What dimension do you think myth adds? I could walk into a room with a group of kids and do group psychotherapy, work with the energies of the people in the room in much the same way that you're describing that you do. But you've got that other presence of the myth there. Can you talk about what that adds?

MEADE: Well, the myth adds vitality. You know, *vita*—life. Myths connect us back to the core of life. They're about beginnings in one direction, and core centrality in another. They make vital energy available. Kids get it right away. This is not Disney. And this is not history. Something mysterious is moving here.

The second thought that comes to mind is that it has a transcendent quality. So, myth brings the Unseen into the room. It brings in the Invisibles. I'm telling the story of a half-boy. Well, I didn't say whether it was half-top or half-bottom—I didn't say. Everybody has to image his or her own half-boy. So, the population of the room has just multiplied. Not only doubled, because it's only half. *(laughter)* It's multiplied in a strange and provocative way. And everybody feels it. The room is bigger. Kids say, "Boy, that's the best day I ever had in school." And they can't say why. But the room was full of imagination, it was full of images, and therefore it was full of psycho-emotional-mental vitality.

Myth can transcend to other levels in other contexts. I'll work with gangs, and they'll be throwing hand signs. I'll say, "You understand where that comes from?"

They'll say, "What do you mean?"

I say, "Where using signs comes from?"

They say, "Yeah, it comes from the 'hood.'"

I say, "Let's talk about where it comes from before the 'hood' was the 'hood.'"

They'll say, "What do you mean?"

And I say, "Well, originally, the fingers were used to communicate. Your sign identifies your group, but you can get a lot more sophisticated. If we wanted to get into it, we could have a language no one else knows. We could all talk secretly by using our fingers, very subtly, and no one would know what we were saying, except those of us who knew the language. Signs come from finger and body languages."

They go, "Really? Where'd they do that?"

"Well, they did it in Ireland, they did it in Africa."

Someone will say, "That's cool. What else?"

I say, "Well, that's organized signs, but your body's always giving signs."

Someone says, "What do you mean?"

I say, "I've noticed that you're always tapping on your knee. The two people on either side of you aren't tapping on their knees, so we could get into the signs you're giving us about who you are and what you're feeling."

So they're caught into it, if it's working. In a matter of minutes we've gone from the posture and defensive thing of the gang signs to prehistory and body language, if they want to go that way, or we're doing the origin of speech and language and the use of fingers. Often, I'll use the idea of five fingers and five senses to open ideas of being in the cosmos.

It seems to me that one of the biggest problems a young person has is figuring out where they fit. Usually they think, "*Do* I fit?" But it's really *where* do they fit. To fit is to be cosmologically aligned. That's what it really means; cosmos is the order where everything fits. When I get to where I fit, then I'm cosmologically connected. To me, there can be more self-esteem in that than years of therapy. It gets right to the core of the situation. I'm working with the possibility that people have cosmological longings and feelings. I do. So I figure that they might. *(laughter)* That would also be a transcendent moment, when someone suddenly says, "Wow, I get who I am."

So, I think that myth adds the unseen; it adds vitality that is not overtly there otherwise. It adds a transcendent function, a cosmological connection. Those are the three things I think of.

HANSEN: You say that myth adds a transcendent function. I'm thinking of Jung's notion of the transcendent function. I'm wondering, are you talking about the unconscious?

MEADE: I'm talking about the great unconscious, or the great unseen, if you wanted to say it more mythologically, the unconscious being more of a psychological term. The Irish would call it the Other World. Now, my job, working with any young people, is to open doors that allow the Other World to be present, and to say this is how we really are when we're people. Sometimes I'll say it outright, but sometimes I'll just be alluding to it. So, that's transcendent, because it gives them more awareness that they're connected to some unseen world, which everybody's been talking about since the origin of time. It's often everybody except the people teaching them. So, I'll try to show them that there's another world, the inner-under-other world. I do that when I say, "Once upon a time..." I'm saying, "We're going to turn now to the direction where stories come from, where unseen things live." You know, they get it. They all get it.

HANSEN: I felt the hypnotic part of that. It was kind of a hypnotic suggestion.

MEADE: Yes, and it involves a shift of attention and rhythm. Traditionally it is called light trance. Which is the same thing they're getting from putting their CD and earphones on; they're going into light trance. It's just that this trance is transcendent. Whereas the other one may be or may not be.

HANSEN: Do you personally experience myth as psychoactive? Can you describe an experience when myth was helpful to you psychologically?

MEADE: I'm a very fortunate person, because I tell stories on a regular basis. And the way I tell a story is not a recitation; the story is different every time I tell it. When I first told stories, I tried to recite. I knew something was wrong. I just happened to be playing a drum one day, and then started telling a story while playing the drum. At that moment, the story awakened for me. While telling a story, I'm actually seeing it in unbelievable detail, much more than I could convey verbally. The experience that I have is as if there are two flows, or two streams coming up and rolling across the tongue. One is a memory stream, where I'm remembering the story, hopefully. *(laughter)* I used to worry about that, and getting the parts of the story right, not necessarily exact, but in the rough shape that they need to be in for the story to be all right. And then the other stream involves what's happening in that room in that moment, what's up for the group and for me. The words—I don't know which words will be shaped by those two flows.

HANSEN: So, the energy in the room is channeling through you then.

MEADE: Yeah, it's a mixture of that, and memory. I try to let it go as freely as possible. While it's happening, I am having a psychoactive experience. It's strong enough that for the first six years I was doing it, I couldn't comment or talk about the story immediately afterwards. I would have to let the audience talk and just nod my head while I gathered myself, or if I was working with someone else, I would ask them to comment and then I would gather myself to come back to be able to say something.

HANSEN: You would gather yourself from where? Where were you in your experience that you couldn't talk?

MEADE: In that kind of psychoactively mythic space. I was still in the story. I'd come to the end of the story, but the story was still going in me. I always say, if you pay attention to the story a certain thing will strike you, and that's the best thing to go with. But that's happening to me too. And so I would still be there. It would be almost like a mythic hangover; I would be stuck in the story and unable to deal with the audience. I had to learn how to make that shift. Now, I'm still in that space to some degree, but part of me takes an in-between ground where I can hear what people are saying, and stay in touch with what's going on within me. Usually. Previously I couldn't hold the ground in-between, I'd need five, six, seven minutes to get myself together.

Hansen: Do you think it would be safe to assume that's happening for many of the people in the room?

Meade: Yes, it is happening. But it was confusing, because it was also happening to me.

Hansen: I understand.

Meade: It would be as if the patient came in and said, "I'm feeling terrible," and the therapist said, "You're feeling terrible, whoa, you should see how I feel!" I was in that state. I mean, psychoactive. I was *way* activated.

Hansen: Do you ever comment on your own process as a way of bridging being with yourself and being with the audience?

Meade: Not usually. Sometimes. If I've forgotten a piece of the story, I certainly will say, "I left something out." That tells me that's the part I need to pay attention to. So, I want to now pay attention to it. Because I didn't say it, no one else can pay attention to it, so I'll have to do that. But if that hasn't happened, then I may or I may not. I'll say things about the story. But I have learned, or at least I feel strongly, that for people to have a chance to say where they are in a psychoactive sense is so valuable these days, that I'll try to get that to happen. Now, if people in the room are *not* having this psychoactive experience, because they've been overly educated or whatever has happened, then sometimes I will have to help it along.

Hansen: How do you do that?

Meade: If a group is resistant to the psychoactive aspect of a story and the mythic qualities present in it, then I feel I have to engage that and crack it open somehow so those who are able to feel can hold onto what they have. I'm aware of the psychoactive part of myth and how it can be interfered with. I should also mention that I tell stories usually because the story psychoactively grabs me. Someone will say, "What story are you going to tell?" I don't know yet. It's not because I'm not paying attention, it's that the story hasn't shown up. So, the whole thing starts psychoactively for me. Often, there's some image that suggests: *tell this story*. And I've learned to watch how that gets confirmed. *(laughter)* So, to me, the whole thing is psychoactive.

Hansen: You're working with altered states of consciousness.

Meade: Stories do that. Language itself does that. I love language and listen closely to what people say. I'll try to crack words open and say, "Here's what I thought you said." Young people love that.

Hansen: What happens when someone has a large emotional response? When a teenager has a large emotional response to where he finds his place in the myth, and it's perhaps painful or traumatic, how do you handle that?

Meade: I go with it. I confirm that, too. I was working with a group of Native American kids. One girl got very upset. I noticed it, and so I said, "Do you want to say something, because you haven't said where you were in the story." She shook her head, but her body was saying, *yes I do*. So I said, "Well, you don't have to, but at any point that you want to, you could say it."

Someone else said, "No, she won't say it, but we all know what's wrong with her."

So I thought, *okay, that's why she's shaking her head; she's already been shut down.* So I said, "Well, if you know what's wrong with her, if you really do, you wouldn't say it that way. Because if you knew what was wrong with her, as you say, you'd have more sympathy, because it's probably very similar to what's wrong with you." The room becomes tense.

And someone says, "What are you saying?"

I said, "I'm saying we all have something wrong with ourselves, and usually we all get it rejected. I want to say again to Sally, that if you want to say anything, I'd love to hear it, and if anybody gives you a hard time, I'll take care of that."

So, she started crying. Then she said, "They took my baby away."

And I said, "Why?"

She totally broke down. And someone else said, "'cause she was beating it." They took her baby away for child abuse.

I said, "Come on, don't talk like that." So we had to get into this whole tragedy that was happening on the reservation. She couldn't take it. She had to leave. So I asked some women to go with her. There was a concern that we had overdone it. We all talked about it for quite a while. We got into the aspect that on the reservation there was a lot of abuse.

I said, "Look, how many of you have been abused?" I said, "Let's put our hands up." All the hands went up. So now we're into the pain everyone brought into the room.

The next day, we're back together and who shows up but Sally.

So I said, "Are you okay?"

She said, "I'm fine."

I said, "I hope that wasn't too painful. I hope I didn't do something out of order."

She said, "I needed that." She said, "I feel better." And she looked around clearly at everybody. You can get in trouble that way, but what I've learned is that if there's a story in the room, there are answers as well as problems. Stories make a shape: a beginning, middle, and an end. Most of life doesn't have that. I've learned that a lot of risks can be taken. Even in that case, I had told them a story. I pulled them back to the story.

I said, "Don't you see how that was like the story?"

17

HANSEN: Do you offer the story for some problem-solving ideas? For people to see: what did so-and-so do with this problem, when he only had half a self?

MEADE: Oh, yeah, we get into that. But usually they want to take it in directions that they're seeing themselves. It seems to me that the vitality of myth invites emotion, so I go with the emotions that try to enter. I figure the emotion is the evidence that something vital and possibly transcendent is going on. So, I figure we're going to ride it. I always thank anybody who puts the emotion in, whatever it is. I've had kids get real upset. "What the hell's that?" Question things. Get angry. But it's good, though. Stories can take it. The story's 9,000 years old. It's been kicked around before.

HANSEN: So you just keep affirming, affirming, affirming whoever and whatever shows up.

MEADE: Yeah. Unless I'm in bad shape, I do. *(laughter)* Because I think what myth is trying to do is to make things be fully present: present mentally, psychologically, emotionally, and spiritually. I think that's what's trying to happen, and actually I feel it. That's where it's psychoactive to me. I feel bigger, more openhearted. I mean, I get caught in all kinds of places, and have all kinds of weak moments, but generally speaking, for me, in the presence of a story I feel bigger, I feel we're all going to be better and have more options.

HANSEN: How do you close the storytelling? I feel I have a sense of how you open and how you're working with the energy of the people in the room. How do you bring closure for that time, and what do you hope to leave the kids with?

MEADE: Well, I use a lot of songs and little ceremonies. You can have all kinds of things happen, especially with young people. Stories are provocative. You can tell—there are a couple kids over there on the verge of tears; a couple kids over here have already heard more than they can handle. Because something will hit so fast, so hard, that they'll either have to leave or shut down. The drumming is extremely helpful. If there's a lot of resistance and for whatever reasons it's not easy for them to sing, I will do something where I just play the drums faster and faster. What

I'm doing is gathering them into the rhythm, and I'll just go faster and faster until they're wondering, "Can he go any faster?" And they don't realize they've let go of everything. I'm just giving it a crescendo, and then it's a big release. It's like a small ritual, through the drum. So I'll do things like that.

If it's possible we'll try to all do something. I'll have everybody shake hands, or a little closure thing so they know it's over. Although if you can get them to sing, then there's a hidden, understandable message that we have a little harmony, everything's okay. See, the thing is the stories start at a certain place, go through trouble, and come out all right. So, they're contained. All I have to do is repeat the ending back to them, that it comes out okay.

HANSEN: How do you do that?

MEADE: Well I might talk to them about the end. If it's a group of young people, at the beginning I'll tell them that life is hard, and that I know that it's harder now. Then at the end, I can say something like, our job is to come closer to living our own story. It doesn't mean that we'll be happy every day, but it does mean that we'll come out at the end having been ourselves, and that's the best thing we can do. I'll somehow reinforce that at the end. I'll usually make it out of the moment, a high moment, or like in the case of that young woman, Sally, who had to run out. It turned out to be a big story throughout the whole reservation, about what had happened. Everybody already knew she had been abused in her family. Everybody knew what it was about. At the end of the first day, I pulled a candle out of my bag and said, "I'm going to put this candle down, and I'm going to ask you to sing a song with me, and I'm going to light this candle. We're going to be singing for Sally, that something eases the burden in her heart and that she doesn't hurt herself. Maybe she's made a mistake, but also people did that to her. And to us." And the reservation kids, half of them are rolling their heads. So I said, "If you can't participate, then I ask you to be respectful enough not to interfere." It's usually the guys who are a problem, and I've dealt with their resistance early on, usually, engaged them, so if they get too much, I just look at them or tell them, "Just be quiet for a while." But usually they're into it, because they know the pain as well. So we ended the day that way.

At the end of the next day they said to me, "What are you going to do at the end?" They learn so fast. Well, I brought a candle for everybody that day. I said, "We're all going to light a candle and hope that the flames of all our lives keep going a long time. But there's one in the middle, and I'd like Sally to light that one, and then we're all going to light ours from hers." So then I'm showing them that the broken part is where the healing begins; that she had the courage to start it. I'm not saying anything, but they understand. Sally's been given a place of honor because she was brave enough to say what she had to say.

HANSEN: You intuitively weave the myth with the personal stories in the room.

MEADE: I think that the only way people get myths is through the deeply personal.

HANSEN: Because...?

MEADE: We talk about myth in a knowing way. I deal with a lot of audiences who have no idea of what I'm doing. Yet, they feel it. They go along with it, but I can't use words like "psychoactive," and I can't say "transcendent," or I'd lose half the audience. So, it's fun to talk about it with you. I spend a lot of time writing and thinking about it myself. I wish I had been more encouraged in my own education. I got the taste for it at age thirteen. Thankfully.

HANSEN: From Aunt...?

MEADE: Florence. Yeah. My Aunt Florence. A little devout Catholic woman. She never had any idea what it was about either. I tried to thank her once. I really think that if there were one thing that could be applied to the culture, that's the thing I would apply.

HANSEN: Myth?

MEADE: Mythic perspective or 'mythic sense,' I'm calling it lately. The mythic sense is what's missing. It's the antidote to literalism. It's the extension and deepening of psychological work. Myth recreates the communal, and it recreates the connection to the invisible. You know, the Irish used to say, *what's wrong in this world can only be healed by the*

20

Other World. And what's wrong in the Other World can only be healed by this world. They think the Other World gets out of whack too. I've always loved that idea, that if you're bringing myth into a situation in an honest way, you are doing something that benefits both worlds. I'm not all that positive a person in some regards, yet I've become more so as I've gotten older. I've always been positive about that—the presence of the Other World. I've just seen it. And it works for me, makes me feel more vital. Therefore I'm more alert to vitality in other people. I'm more alert to where the vitality in the situation is, where the psychoactive part resides.

Which symbol is striking now? As a storyteller you can tell rather quickly. Then if you add certain kinds of songs, from them you can also read the mood and the nuance in the group. With any kind of luck you can actually be helping move the energy in revealing and healing ways. So, I think the mythic perspective is a wonderful thing, and I think it's really the missing thing in the culture. We listen to governmental leaders and all the maniacal stuff they're into. They use incredibly dull language to talk about medicine—healing is not mentioned. Everything has been reduced to the lowest level of what it could be. Living imagination isn't in the language or in the thought. I think an understanding, and even an intuitive grasp of myth, in almost all cases, improves the situation.

Myth helps young people in particular, because they are trying to find out who they are. And who they are is mythic by nature. That's the old idea, and I think it's still the best idea. It confounds some of the things that they've been force-fed. To be mythic is to participate in nobility. That's how I understand it. There's a noble quality just because it's mythic. It may be tragic, but it has nobility. That's another thing that can be communicated quite quickly, and then confirmed.

I don't know how else you do that. You can't tell a group of young people in general, "Gee—you're great." They're all thinking, *which part of being great am I?* That's what they need to know. A myth or a story, or something that gives a mythic framework or a mythic loom, it does that.

They will automatically and immediately pick the spot in the myth that is related to where their core images are. They will. They'll cross gender boundaries to get to the core images, they'll cross all they've been force-fed, they'll transcend age, class, even religion. It's a cool thing.

HANSEN: I thank you for sharing your sense of your work.

MEADE: You're welcome.

HANSEN: It's beautiful to hear you talk about what you do. You really invoke the mythic realm and bring it into the room. I got carried into it just listening to you. I also really like how you amplify the resonant field between collective myth and personal psyche. The vibrations between myth and the psychological are so expansive.

MEADE: Oh, yeah. The psychological stuff gets quite revealed. I'll tell you the truth. I've had to hold back on a lot of it. You can do physical diagnosis if you want. I have a process where I'll have each person take a place in the story and then everybody's *in* the story, and we retell the story to each other. But not just feeding back the story. Each person figures out why they're in that place by discussing it with others that are nearby. Now they've inhabited the story. Someone says, "Well, I'm at the place in the story where the girl finally speaks, and the reason I'm here is because for some reason when I was twelve years old I started to stutter." Then, the whole story comes out, and usually tears, and all this unresolved inner stuff, because I ask them to find memories and emotions. Then I'll say, "Okay, and why are you there now?" And usually there's an *"Oh my goodness,"* because I'm back in a place similar to that, and I no longer stutter, but I'm going back and forth without going anywhere in my life. In my relationship I'm stuck: I can't leave and I can't stay.* You know, just incredible gushing out. About the second time I ever did that, I was doing it intuitively; I was telling a story, and this man was talking off the point. His words were disconnected from his body. I was just looking at him, and I said, "Do you have an intestinal problem?" And he said, "What do you mean?" I said, "I'm just wondering if you have digestive problems," since his words came out completely empty. I looked at his body.

HANSEN: You looked at his body and saw what?

MEADE: Well, I can't claim. Since he wasn't saying anything that had either any emotion or any insight in it, I couldn't listen, so I just watched. As I was watching, I was thinking, he's at a really odd place in the story, he's the only one there, and here's what the story is about at that point. It just dawned on me: this guy's got some kind of intestinal issue. So I asked him, and he said, "I got diagnosed three days ago with intestinal cancer." He said, "I haven't even told anybody. How do you know that?" I said, "Just where you are in the story." We talked a little bit later, and he really wanted me to explain it, and I couldn't explain it. It's happened to me a number of times.

HANSEN: It's intuitive.

MEADE: Yeah. Also, the story is like an x-ray. You can see things. And I think it's even a matter of how much you want to see. I don't particularly want to see that. I don't find that to be the most useful. So I don't try to do it. I don't know what would happen if I tried to do it. But, to me it's that powerful. There is a revelatory quality to all mythic things, and it can happen on many, many levels. I remember that was really shocking to me. Because everybody was saying afterwards, "Where did that come from?" I said, "I don't know! I'm just trying to pay attention. I had this idea so I thought I'd say it."

HANSEN: It seems like part of what happens when you're telling the story and working with the group is that the story opens you—you become an open channel for the story and the people in the room.

MEADE: I have to be to tell the story. I just try to learn to go: *okay, the door's open, let's see what we'll find.*

HANSEN: You open to all sorts of knowledge, awareness, that in normal, day-to-day walking around we don't access.

MEADE: The good thing about story, I think, is because of its beginning, middle, and end, it can hold anything, and you can do so much with it. It's a very bold arena, because it has its own intelligence. I learn *directly* from stories. I remember having this argument with some academics. I said something, and they asked, "Where does that idea come from?" I said, "The story." They said, "No, no, you had to have read that." *(laughter)* Story means storehouse. Things are stored in there, and they can come to you directly. You could write the things down and then you could publish them if you want, but they come directly. That's what I've learned. It's not only psychoactive. Myth is also a direct educational tool that will teach you. The Irish say one of the Gaelic words for "to teach" is "to sing over." I think that stories sing over people. More and more that's how I go with it. The story's now going to sing over us, and we're going to learn something from its song.

HANSEN: Beautiful.

MEADE: Yeah, it's amazing to find something that you can love and trust. That's what it's like for me. I feel really grateful about the whole thing. Increasingly, I think I'm more, not always, but often more awake to it. I try to seize the time to enter mythic space. We must enter it right now. This is it. After this comes airports, all the things I have to do, but for this period of time we have a 'mythic sense' to work with. And therefore things can make sense.

I think that it's great that you're studying myths. Young people are waiting right there. They're mythic. They're in their own mythic spell. They just don't know it. Myth is great for kids; with it they feel they fit in. They feel more confirmed in the world.

CHAPTER TWO

Interview with
Betty Staley

Betty Staley

Betty Staley has taught for over thirty years in Steiner Waldorf schools, including nineteen years as a high school teacher. For the last twelve years, she has taught at Rudolf Steiner College, where she directs the Foundation Year, the Summer Waldorf High School Teacher Education Program, the Public School Institute, and the Professional Development Program for Teachers of At-Risk Students. Staley has developed curriculum in myth and taught myths extensively.

She is the author of five books: *Ow and the Crystal Clear*; *Between Form and Freedom: A Practical Guide to the Teenage Years*; *Hear the Voice of the Griot: A Celebration of African History, Geography, and Culture*; *Tapestries: Weaving Life's Journey*; and *Soul Weaving*. Her latest book, *Adolescence, the Sacred Passage: Insights from the Story of Parzival,* is in production. Staley has lectured worldwide, most recently in Japan, where her topic "Overcoming the Crisis in Adolescence" was inspired by the Japanese translation of *Between Form and Freedom*.

MAREN HANSEN: So, to start, can you give me a summary of what you do here at the Rudolf Steiner College?

BETTY STALEY: During the academic year, I direct the Foundation Studies Program. This program is a general introduction to the ideas of Rudolf Steiner, to inner development, and to an immersion in the arts as a means of self-transformation. It also serves as the first year of a two-year Waldorf teacher-training program.

In the summer, I am particularly busy, because I direct Foundation Studies for high school teachers and for elementary school teachers in foreign languages and handwork, as well as the High School Teacher Education Program and the Public School Institute.

HANSEN: That's a lot. I'm curious, for the Waldorf teacher training, is that a Masters Degree level? Do people have a B.A. already when they come in?

STALEY: Most do, although some of them will do a B.A. completion while they're with us.

Hansen: I know that you are doing some work with juvenile delinquents. Tell me about that.

STALEY: Well, we work with young people ages ten to eighteen. For the past nine years, a colleague and I have been working with a court and community school in Marysville, California. We are adapting the Waldorf approach to the education of juvenile delinquents. This program has been very successful, and we have received grants to do professional development workshops for California teachers working with at-risk youngsters. I've been a bridge builder between independent Waldorf education and public initiatives. So, I've been involved with training staffs and giving talks and working with the school districts. And I still teach one block in the Waldorf School for the 12th grade.

HANSEN: What do you teach?

STALEY: Russian Literature. Until last year, I also taught a course named Symptomatology, a course in the development of consciousness. We survey the history, science, and philosophy the students have studied throughout their school years, and then focus on contemporary issues that concern the students most. I also introduce them to Freud, Jung, and Steiner in this course. It's the first official time they hear about Steiner, and so I compare ideas. It's their last course before they perform their senior play and graduate.

HANSEN: Tell me about your role in working with the mythological curriculum in the high school.

STALEY: In 1976, I developed a course in mythology for ninth graders. Since then, I have changed it many times. I had been teaching history of art in the ninth grade, and a particular freshman class had a number of students who had not been in the school in the earlier years. They didn't have the background in myths that students who have attended Waldorf Schools all the way through generally have. I felt I could not really do justice to art history unless the students had some idea of the mythical characters, such as Prometheus, Athena, and Jupiter. So, I developed the course. The faculty felt it helped the students, so it has become part of the curriculum ever since.

I was interviewing a student one time who was applying to come into the high school, and I mentioned that myth would be my first block. She said, "Oh, I know all about that." What was interesting was that she had it all down—she was taught to do it the way you parse a sentence. So, you take a myth and you analyze it. What I found lacking in her approach was any emotional relationship whatsoever. It was like a mathematical formula, and that alerted me to how we'd be doing it in a very different way, with a different goal. So, that is another way of teaching myth— from an analytical point of view. It becomes very much a formula.

HANSEN: When you are teaching myth to adolescents, what do you hope to achieve?

STALEY: First, the most obvious thing is to teach them myths so that they become aware that myths exist and that they exist all over the world. People have been making up myths since the beginning of time. Then, next is to evoke in the students a kind of curiosity as to why human beings make up myths. What is it about the human being that we not only have myths that have been passed down, but we make up myths all the time? What are some of the myths that you've grown up with? Or what are some of the myths that live in America? They always think about George Washington and the cherry tree, and Santa Claus, and so on. And then we'll use those later: "How is that myth touching you at different life stages?" Then, of course, I always ask, "What are the myths that you know?" If they're Waldorf students, there are lots of myths that they know. A question I have about the work you are doing with a myth curriculum is: How broadly are you defining myth? Are you including the fairy tale, for example? I mean, I would. Would you include the Old Testament and New Testament in a study of myths?

HANSEN: You know Joseph Campbell's statement—that myths are other people's religions.

STALEY: *(laughter)* I think there's a lot of truth to that. So anyway, that would be a question when you design a curriculum. Then, another reason to teach myth to adolescents is to stimulate their sense that they can find patterns, that there's orderliness in life. This is very much a Waldorf approach to phenomenology. Rather than giving them the answer, you evoke the question and let them come up with the answer. So, instead of saying, "Find the flood in these five myths," the teacher would say, "You read those myths last night, what did you find in common?" Then, the answers come from them: "It was somebody who was wise," "somebody who had to go through many tests," and so on. Then as the weeks evolve they say, "There are patterns in myths from all over the world." So they begin to pull out what these patterns are. And that, I think, is really important, because it's a picture—just at this adolescent stage—that there is orderliness in chaos. I think that's important to see. But not going so far that it becomes a formula. I think it has to be kept living.

Another reason to teach myth is that there are different levels in the way that we understand things. Usually about the third day of the course, the students say, "Are these myths true?" That is the perfect opportunity to talk about truth existing on many levels. I draw a diagram with seven curved lines. In each one, I write a level of truth. For example, the first level has to do with the level of a story. Other levels have to do with the truth in social interaction, in historical facts, in geography, truth in the soul, in symbols, archetype, and spirit. I introduce them to the word archetype, but in ninth grade, what they tend to come up with most are stereotypes. And so then you'd say, "What's the difference between a

28

stereotype and an archetype?" We're planting seeds. In tenth grade, when they hear about Plato, they meet the term archetype again. Then I've had the joy of being able to teach these same students in twelfth grade and come to some of these same issues, and they have a different consciousness.

By studying myths, students begin to understand that stories have been told for generations because myths help people understand something about their own lives. That's the beginning of the psychological level. High school students enjoy experiencing the imagination in myths, and relate the images to their own lives. They see that they can learn something from myths, no matter how old they are. You can hear the same myths over and over again, and each time the meaning is different and deeper.

HANSEN: How do you convey to your high school students that the myth is something that they can bring into their own lives to help them?

STALEY: Well, for example, let's take the myth of Gilgamesh. You can tell that myth in the fifth grade, as we do in the Waldorf School. They paint scenes, draw scenes, and act out the myths, and we leave it there. We don't analyze it. In high school, they read the myth, and then we look at the patterns and say, "What were the big issues here?" The students might say, "Gilgamesh is restless, and because he's restless he's keeping everybody working." The idea of friendship is an important issue. Then there's the big one—you know, when Enkidu is humanized and leaves the forest, the animals no longer recognize him. Another issue is the facing of the monster, Humbaba. These are the big issues in this myth.

I'll ask: "Does any of this resonate with you in your life?" Then the answers come: "He was completely one with the animals, and they accepted him." And then what started to happen, of course, is he started to have his hair combed, he started to drink and eat and become human. There is a time when the lion comes down and attacks the sheep, and Enkidu goes out to greet him because he knows the lion. He goes out and wrestles it, but the lion doesn't recognize him. Enkidu's response is to fall down onto the forest floor and weep and weep and weep. There you have this picture of the loss of innocence. When I was teaching fifth grade I told this story. I had a girl in the class who didn't want to grow up. She just wanted to play. We did this story, and she just drew that scene where Enkidu wept over and over again. At a certain point, she was done. She was ready to let go. I still know her. She's now forty-four years old. I happened to see her a couple of weeks ago. I asked, "Annie, do you remember this?" She said no. She remembered the story, but she has no memory that she drew this scene over and over again. She was fascinated as I told her what I had experienced. The power of myth is that it goes right into the unconscious.

HANSEN: Is that why you don't analyze the myths with the younger grades?

STALEY: Exactly, we leave it free.

HANSEN: When do you change that?

STALEY: Ninth grade.

HANSEN: Oh, that doesn't change until ninth grade? I didn't realize that.

STALEY: There wouldn't be a lot of analysis unless it comes up in conversation. The students feel very free to bring things up, but a teacher wouldn't push it in that direction. It's really with this change into adolescence that we become more conscious. In fact, what happened in this one block was the students said, "We've had a lot of these myths in the elementary school." I said, "Yes, you did." They would even criticize me if the words I used in ninth grade weren't the same as in an earlier grade, so then I talked about different versions. Their memories are so incredible. And then I asked them the question, "What would have happened if we were doing in fifth grade what we're doing now?," which is interpreting the myths. They said, "It would have killed it." That was such an important statement. Telling the story for the story's sake is what you're doing with younger children. You respect that their unconscious is doing what it has to do with it. If you bring it out into analysis, you are killing it. Because, you're really killing the imagination.

HANSEN: How is that different for teenagers and adults?

STALEY: Well, a lot of it has to do with the fact that the awakening of thinking is putting teenagers into the objective world, and they're going back and forth [between unconscious imagination and conscious thought]. Part of the challenge of adolescence is to begin to separate the two worlds, and yet be able to move between the two worlds.

Some students still want to hold on to the story itself, and they resist losing the narrative in order to summarize it. We touch lightly on interpretation in the context of a theme, for example, creation, the path to enlightenment, or the hero's journey. Ninth graders are able to see themes and understand that the stories they loved so much when they were younger have deeper meaning than simply being a good story. As students mature through the high school years, we ask them to think about the story and find meaning in it for themselves. By twelfth grade, many students grasp a deeper level of meaning in myth or other forms of literature.

HANSEN: There's an interesting tension between telling the story and interpreting the story. I've certainly heard people kill myths by interpreting them. Yet, I've also heard people open myths in ways so that they don't lose their power or their magic.

STALEY: Oh, yes, absolutely.

HANSEN: So, what would that difference be?

STALEY: I mentioned that the students said the myths would have been killed if the teacher spoke about the meaning of the myths when they were in elementary school. Children in the elementary school years live in their imaginations, and they relate to stories in an unconscious way. Their feelings are rich and deep. They identify with characters and the events in myths, and it is like food for the soul. If we analyze the myths with elementary school children, we wake them up prematurely. We wake them from their imaginations, and in a sense, we dampen their childlike relationship to the world. Around the ages of eleven or twelve, children's thinking becomes more objective, more related to cause and effect than to imagination. We know this from understanding brain development and also psychological development. The magic of the world is fading, and the world is becoming more objective and factual. Although they continue to love myths, they separate them from reality.

In adolescence, we reintroduce them to myths in a different way. Now, we can acknowledge that the myths are not true in a factual way, but they are true in a deeper way. They are ready to see that truth lives on many levels. However, with the younger child, if you start analyzing the story, rather than enriching it, you close something off. It's like giving the answer instead of raising a question.

HANSEN: In opening a myth with teenagers, and with adults, we acknowledge that there's a difference between letting the magic of the myth still vibrate and what we've both experienced as people killing the myth. What makes the difference?

STALEY: When you avoid giving an interpretation, the myth is still living. The teacher doesn't give one answer, but asks questions that are open-ended. Students are encouraged to come up with their own ideas of what the myth might mean. By having an active discussion, students experience a variety of approaches to the myths and this stimulates their thinking. Everybody's opinion is valid. The myth is killed when it has only one meaning. We know that the beauty of a myth and the reason myths have lasted for so long is because one can continually deepen the meaning of them. As we go through new experiences in our lives, we see new meaning in a myth.

In his lectures to Waldorf teachers, Rudolf Steiner differentiated between the thinking of the child before thirteen or fourteen years of age and after. After this age, children experience an awakening of the soul life, which ranges from the highest ideals to the lowest smut. Over the high school years, teenagers learn how to gain control over the wide range of impulses they experience. As they become more rational and less emotional, they become better masters of their lives.

Plato describes this transition beautifully. He describes a charioteer who is controlling two horses that are pulling the chariot. One horse wants to fly like Pegasus, while the other horse just wants to race along distracted by whatever comes his way. Plato calls the charioteer "the intellectual soul" or "mind soul." The charioteer has to bring the two horses together so that they trot at the same speed. This is the challenge the adolescent faces in using thinking to bring his idealistic thoughts down to earth and focusing his more sensual energy so it doesn't get lost and dissipated.

HANSEN: That is a challenge. It's a wonder any of us make it.

STALEY: *(laughter)* I start the course by giving the students many quotations about myths. The students reflect on various ideas people have had about myths, and this gives them the sense that myths are complicated and special, that they can't be easily figured out. This stimulates wonder in the student. After hearing many ideas, the students then read the myths and come up with their own ideas. A basic principle in Waldorf education is going from the whole to the parts. In other words, an overview, or a context, is given, and then we look at specifics. After reading and discussing specific myths, we then move back to the whole by generalizing what the myths have revealed. This is true also with each individual myth. We look at the whole myth, then we look at the components of it, and put it back together.

HANSEN: That's an important aspect of your teaching style.

STALEY: Yes, very important. That starts right in kindergarten and first grade. For example, they're given a number—say, twenty-four—and they have to come up with all the possible ways of making twenty-four. It's very different from saying what's twelve and twelve, which leaves just one answer. And so we continue carrying multiple possibilities into the high school.

Let's see, what are some other reasons for teaching myths? Another is to introduce moral codes of behavior in different cultures. Through the myths we see, *oh in this myth, this is what's valued—in this other myth, that is what's valued.* You begin to see the myth as the educator of the people in a particular culture, through which they are taking in these social mores. In many Grimm stories you've got the three brothers: one is going to conquer through brute force; the second is going to conquer through his cleverness; and it's always the third one who does it through his heart forces. Now what's the value here? Through the heart you're going to be able to conquer or fulfill trials for which brute force and cleverness by themselves are not enough. That's a real value. Unfortunately, it's not one that's very much taken up by our society. What is it that's being told to the children through those stories over and over again? Lying, jealousy, or envy does not help you gain the treasure.

HANSEN: You're saying that the myth offers a form of ethical teaching.

STALEY: Yes, and cultural learning. Yet, I think it's very important that we move from the cultural level to the universal level. So very important. For example, why are the people in the creation myth from Central America made from corn? Why are they created out of ice in the Norse myths? Students begin to realize that the people used what was around them to explain their world. Myths are a kind of explanation of natural forces. How do you explain the thunder? How do you explain a hurricane? Myths often personify these events and give reasons for them.

"What were some of the myths you came up with as a child when there was thunder and lightning?" Children come up with all kinds of things: "I thought the angels were banging pots." They see that they've been living with myth from their early years.

So we ask, "What were some of the myths you've been living with?," and always Santa Claus comes up. "Let's look at that. When was the first time you discovered Santa Claus wasn't real?" And this is when you really get ninth graders talking. They like to share their experiences. One will say, "I came down and my parents were wrapping presents, and my older sister told me they were giving me the presents, not Santa Claus." They hold the stories.

"Well, and what happened then, when you found out?" They have different answers. "Well, did that make it untrue? Did it make Santa Claus untrue?" Well, no. And then it goes from Santa Claus as a being to Santa Claus as a kind of quality in a person to his being a pure symbol. "What is the quality of Santa Claus?"

"Well, my mom said it that it was like, you know, generosity," and so on. So we still call him Santa Claus, but we know that our parents are giving the presents to us. And then over time we don't need to have the image of Santa Claus anymore because it is just—well—people give each other things because they care for each other. And then the students want to bring up the Tooth Fairy and the Easter Bunny. This is when the ninth graders are on fire. We have a lot of laughter as they recall specific situations around the Tooth Fairy or the Easter Bunny. And yet it is a precious moment as they reflect on how different they were as children,

34

compared to now. This is one of the most helpful things for them to see: how myths have evolved in human history, how they can change and lose their importance when they aren't satisfying on a mythic level anymore. But, they can still live on as good stories.

HANSEN: Stories that are woven into their souls.

STALEY: Yes. From a very practical, academic point of view I let them know that the great myths of the world are a foundation for literature, for history, for art, and that they will know them for the rest of their lives. Myths have practical meaning for practical kids. For example, you're going between Scylla and Charybdis. Here are the two rocks that Odysseus's men had to go between. What is it in our lives when we have two rocks blocking our way and we have to find our way through? We go from speaking about the specific image of the two boulders to talking about the things I have to pass between in my life. It may be that I have to go between different distractions that keep me from finishing my homework, or I'm on the basketball team, but I need to earn money. We try to differentiate between having two simple obstacles or big, threatening obstacles that would more closely resemble the image of Scylla and Charybdis. Critical thinking is being exercised.

HANSEN: Yes.

STALEY: And myths are just good fun. I also like young people to know that there are people around the world who have taken myths very seriously and have studied them. I convey this with quotations—a Steiner quote, or a Campbell quote, and so on. They'll choose their favorite quote about mythology, and then they'll write what they think it means. For example, I give them a sheet with, maybe, twenty different quotes about myths. And then, I say, which one do you like the best? Why don't you choose one and write a paragraph about it.

HANSEN: Oh, and then what happens?

STALEY: They talk about it in discussion or they write about it, whatever they choose—they're choosing one that makes sense to them, and then they're taking rather erudite language and adapting it into their own words. For example, there's one that says the myth lifts the veil, the curtain, and we'll talk about this.

Another thing with ninth and tenth graders—you can't take anything for granted. You have to work with the material before you can have them really come to something. That's part of teaching. I'm hoping that they are just going to love myths and want them to be in their lives. I'm hoping that they see that myths have meaning and can teach them something about cultures, and can teach them something about themselves.

HANSEN: Beautiful! How do you think the study of myth relates to human psychological development?

STALEY: That's a wonderful question. Well, they are definitely related. Myths describe development in picture form. For example, the psychological development of leaving childhood. That's something that every child goes through, and whether it's leaving home to go to kindergarten, or day care, or to study abroad, it's scary. There are many, many myths, as well as fairy tales, about going out into the world to seek your fortune. What does that mean?

Another theme I discuss is the creation of masculine and feminine. In looking at some of the myths, how does the girl overcome the obstacles and bring back the treasure? What is it she has to do? What does the boy have to do? How are they different? In myths, the girl doesn't usually go out into the world to gain her fortune. She has the task of understanding relationships. She has to develop things out of her self. She doesn't have to travel far away. She's usually tested in patience and loyalty. Some of the ninth graders understand what is being expressed in these myths. We get to talk about this and also discuss what changes are occurring in current times between the way boys and girls are treated and how they go about learning from life.

In twelfth grade, the conversation has a very different level because the students are ripe for such discussions. For example, they might speak about the differences in how a boy or girl responds after a date. The girls call their best friends to discuss every detail. What do the boys do? Usually, nothing. They may see someone the next day and have a brief conversation. They don't usually get on the phone and say, this is what happened and what do you think he meant and what do you think he thought he meant and, and, and.

This can lead into a conversation about the different ways boys and girls, men and women, approach life. We might look at some psychological studies as well. Ninth graders don't usually express much interest in the details. As soon as one gets a conversation going, they often get stuck in stereotypes and have difficulty understanding archetypes. Yet, it's still of value to introduce the topic even if they can't go very deeply at this time.

Another theme in which myth reflects psychological development is the conflict between good and evil. There comes a time in our lives when we have to make choices. Many myths deal with the theme of choice, of relationship to authority, and overcoming authority. The myth I love to use for that is Prometheus. Think about when Prometheus was told by the gods, "You cannot give fire to human beings." What does this mean? We look at it afresh. What happened before people had fire? Well, they had to eat raw food or go to bed when it was dark. So, Prometheus steals fire from the gods and gives it to human beings, something that's forbidden. What are humans able to do with fire? Well, they can cook, and—ah, they can make weapons! They can forge metals. What's wrong with that? Well, they can kill each other. And, well, we can have atomic bombs. Oh, so was it a good thing that the gods told Prometheus that he wasn't supposed to give fire to human beings? Sounds like a good thing. Yes, he had to give fire to human beings because we have to learn from our mistakes. We have to have freedom. Then they're on fire again. They are discussing something very close to them. Whenever this comes up, they want to speak about how they need their parents to give them more freedom. They never give us enough freedom, my mother never lets me—they get into all that. So what does this all mean? Well, it has something to do with being responsible. Why didn't the gods just trust that human beings could be responsible? Well, you have to be responsible at a certain age. You know, you can't be given the same responsibilities when you're ten that you can when you're fourteen. So, then the ninth graders consider that maybe it's too early to have certain responsibilities. Did Prometheus take fire too early? Wel-l-l, I'm glad he did it! Then we look at the fact that Prometheus was punished for taking fire from the gods and giving it to human beings. Was it a good thing Prometheus gave us fire, or not?

Of course the students argue over it. But he got punished for it. Yes, but it was helpful to humanity. He sacrificed himself. Then we discuss sacrifice. We look at the punishment he was given: this terrible, terrible experience of being chained to the mountains of Caucasus and having his liver eaten out every day by an eagle. Was it worth the sacrifice? Yes, because he would be free one day. What does his name mean? "Pro-me-theus" means "far-seeing." He knew that one day he would be free. He would be freed by somebody who did it not out of obligation, but out of freedom and compassion. This is what Heracles did later on. Prometheus is able to withstand his terrible punishment because he knows what will happen in the future. It's a marvelous story.

Then you could take the myth about Epimetheus, the brother of Prometheus. His name means "seeing in the past." The myth about Epimetheus is the one that includes Pandora, the girl who has the beautiful urn. She had been told not to look inside. Out of curiosity, she looks inside, and all the imps fly out except for hope, which is caught under the lid. This myth deals with questions of curiosity and disobedience, something teenagers can relate to. These myths have to do with psychological development and soul life. They're just wonderful for that.

HANSEN: Do you have a written curriculum of the myths that you teach to the high school students?

STALEY: Well, I have my outline of what I did for the ninth grade block on mythology. As I said earlier, we sat together as a faculty discussing the need for a block that summarizes the myths and also takes them to another level, and then I developed that block. Then we also put the Old Testament and New Testament into the high school curriculum so that the students could understand those images when they see them in life.

In this course I introduce themes of creation, division of unity into male and female, and the hero's journey—the call, obstacles, trials, overcoming obstacles, reaching the goal, and bringing the treasure back to the community. Also, the sacred marriage, paths of enlightenment, good and evil, initiation—that's a very, very important concept in mythology—, death and rebirth, and images of the future. It's a pretty intense three weeks.

HANSEN: Indeed! How do the Waldorf teachers learn all of those myths?

You train the Waldorf teachers to teach that ninth grade curriculum, right?

STALEY: Well, I teach it in the High School training, but the teachers choose their myths.

HANSEN: They don't use your curriculum?

STALEY: They may use it or not. The curriculum is just ideas, and teachers choose what they feel is right for the class, or come up with their own way to teach myths. It's very exciting to see what people come up with. When I first began teaching mythology, I used a book by Padraic Colum, called *Myths of the World*. Colum is a great storyteller. However, the collection didn't have myths from some cultures I wanted to include. I added Native American stories to the course. It is pretty typical in Waldorf teaching that a teacher will be inspired by a colleague's ideas and then go off to develop a new approach. This makes teaching very exciting.

I don't think anyone would say we have a myth curriculum; it's just not as focused as that. I think what we'd say is that the myths come in at different places in the overall curriculum, and in different schools teachers might have a different relationship with myths. Certainly, I have a more psychological approach, and so I have developed that consciously for the full year. Mythology opens up the ninth grade year. When the students come to study tragedy and comedy in literature later in ninth grade, they'll learn additional myths that were written in dramatic form, and in Art History, they'll be looking at myths shown in the visual arts.

In the tenth grade, when the students study ancient history, they'll again be coming to the myths as part of knowing—that's more cultural. For example, in the study of Mesopotamia, they will renew their acquaintance with the epic of Gilgamesh, which they had learned in fifth grade. In the study of ancient Greece, it is fascinating to see how the myths were part of initiation in the mystery centers. For example, the myth of Demeter and Persephone was performed in the mystery center of Eleusis to share the secrets of death and resurrection.

In teaching any historical period, we ask, what is the myth of this particular culture? When you delve deeply into a culture, you come to the myths. These myths are a window into the cultural psyche, and they can also be a way a student can be in touch with certain feelings or experiences in his or her own soul life.

In the eleventh grade, a course on Parzival is taught. Parzival is a medieval legend, but it has many aspects of myth. By eleventh grade, the students are internalizing more of the images they study. We find that by teaching Parzival at this time, spending three weeks on just this story, that it's giving them a real tool. We get analytical with the story. We let the students do the interpreting.

HANSEN: You spend three weeks on the Parzival story? I know this isn't a casual choice, so can you tell me what has gone into choosing that?

STALEY: The biggest mythic focus we have in the three years of high school is the Parzival block. Parzival is usually taught in the eleventh grade because it addresses many of the changes the students are going through at that time. They are beginning to sense there is something higher within them, and their inner life is becoming active. It is as if they are creating a vessel for their higher self to enter. Their sensitivity to a new relationship with the world makes this an exciting age to teach. Of course, some students are more conscious than others. By spending three weeks on the story of Parzival at this age, the students gain tools for reflecting on their own lives. For example, in what ways have they been naive and neglectful of others in their environment? Have they taken responsibility for their behavior, are they able to own their behavior and do something about it? These issues are part of an adolescent's development. The study of Parzival helps them become aware of these situations and offers an imagination of life as initiation.

In Parzival there are many important themes that can be psychoactive, to use your term. One of the first themes is the protective mother trying to hide her son from the dangers of knighthood. Another theme is the way naive boys treat girls, how conscious they are about their actions. Parzival's thinking was so literal that he followed his mother's advice without thinking how relevant it was to a particular situation. A child might say, "My mother told me to do this," but a teenager would have a better way to evaluate a situation.

Another theme is the difference between Gawain, the warm-hearted friend, and Parzival, the loner on a journey. Each has challenges to meet and overcome. Also, each is part of one whole person. In fact, one could say that all the characters are part of one whole person. Each character in the story represents an aspect of ourselves. The brother, Feirefiz, could be the enthusiastic part of ourselves. Sigune, the faithful lover, could be the loyal part of ourselves, and so on.

The highlight of the story is Parzival's maturity to be able to ask the healing question of the Grail King, "Uncle, what ails you?" This step requires maturity, compassion, and empathy.

HANSEN: I am hearing that this course is a deliberate choice to use myth in manner that both reflects and stimulates psychological development. I think it's very exciting.

STALEY: Well, the students are at the age where they can analyze the story and interpret the scenes, especially as the scenes relate to their own experience. When Gawain is gracious and sweet to the young Obilot, exhibiting impressive self-control, he is similar to older high school boys' behaving gallantly around adoring young girls. On the other hand, when Gawain puts his hand on Antikonie's thigh and expresses himself sexually, we are reminded of high school boys who cannot resist temptation or who are more aggressively sexual. Yet, we can see that despite Gawain's shortcomings, he is a noble knight. We can say the same about many high school boys. When eleventh graders work with this story, they can also see the strengths and weaknesses of the noble Gawain.

In the class we can ask, where is Gawain in his development? We would not ask an eleventh grade boy that question directly. It is too invasive. However, they can gain self-knowledge by identifying Gawain's dilemmas in being noble in one moment and out of control the next. A conversation about this can open up questions about appropriate behavior. Boys are trying to come to terms with their emotions at this time, and such discussions can help them see parallels between the characters and themselves.

HANSEN: Do students share emotionally and out of their personal lives?

STALEY: They feel pretty safe because they've known each other for a long time. But, sometimes knowing each other for a long time can mean that you build up patterns of "I don't feel safe around you." But by and large, our kids are extremely expressive and feel very comfortable. You have to be careful as a teacher that you never abuse that trust. You need to honor that whatever's been told to you is not taken out of the classroom.

HANSEN: As a teacher, you honor a kind of confidentiality—

STALEY: Absolutely.

HANSEN: Well, how do you have the kids do that with each other?

STALEY: I make rules. I say, "We're studying literature. There are things in this story that will bring up personal issues. I want to be clear that we don't gossip about anything that's being said here. I'm making a request of you to honor this. Otherwise classmates will not feel safe, and they will not share." Then it is up to the students. They will often share very delicate feelings. It's up to the teacher not to exploit the situation and pry further. You know, it's not a group therapy session. You don't have that permission. It's not why they're there. You're there to educate them. It's a very fine line and sometimes teachers will go over it. As a teacher you've got to know where you are with that. These moments are private and very precious. If a youngster opens up and shares something private, and for some reason classmates abuse this privacy by either telling others about it or by belittling him or her, the youngster can be devastated. The teacher has to keep the boundaries clear and be attentive to the behavior in the class.

When we study literature we're talking about particular characters, and when you think it relates to your own life, you could choose to share it or keep it to yourself. That leaves a protection there. But, we can discuss situations in the story and explore various options the characters have, leaving the discussion open. I might say: Would anyone like to share something? But I leave it very open. Then somebody would usually share something and we talk about that. I'll say, well, that's something probably a lot of people experience, so let's discuss that for awhile. So you get it away from *who* it is and bring it into the more objective. That's why literature is very good, because it gives you something out there to talk about what's going on in here, rather than, "I want to talk about whether your mother overprotected you." What is so important about the myths and all literature is that they are vicarious, so they're safe.

HANSEN: You are making very clear distinctions between how you, as an educator, handle psychological issues that come up in the classroom, versus how a psychologist in group or individual therapy handles perhaps those very same psychological issues. I think you are right that the agreements in the school setting are different than they are in psychotherapy. I must say that I think you are somewhat unique as an educator, maintaining that psychological discussion and learning does have a place in a school classroom. God knows that there's plenty of research correlating psychological development with cognitive development and a host of psychosocial benefits. But, unfortunately for the students and the society, few schools or teachers seem to understand that.

STALEY: That is unfortunate. What you said about the society reminds me of another important theme in the myth: the return, when the hero brings the treasure, whatever it is, back to the community. The whole idea is that you can't keep it to yourself; your treasure has to be shared. I learned something about this when the students returned from foreign exchanges.

HANSEN: Is that in high school?

STALEY: Yes. Usually at the end of sophomore year or junior year.

HANSEN: I'm surprised that they do foreign exchanges in the sophomore year.

STALEY: It's hard later because of SAT's and college admissions. Students go to different parts of the world, and often when they come back, they are so sophisticated—they've been able to have a drink and they've been able to use good public transportation—and, of course, they feel everybody else is so immature. Meanwhile, their girlfriends or their boyfriends have broken up, and all this stuff has gone on. I was never happy with the way that we teachers handled the return. The students come back from abroad—my own children experienced this too—and the re-entry takes time and has a lot of pain. I realized we weren't setting up the structure for them to give the treasure back to the community. Even if they get up and speak at an assembly in front of their peers, they'll seldom tell serious anecdotes.

Mostly, they're embarrassed and they tell jokes or they diminish the importance of the experience. Especially boys have a hard time sharing something serious or intimate about their experience. They'll find some examples to make their friends laugh. We need to have a place where they feel safe and can share what the importance of the experience was for them. We can invite them to a faculty meeting or set up a lunchtime talk only for those who want to come. When I looked at the stages of the hero in myths, I realized the hero has to give the treasure back to the community. It belongs in the community. By sharing it in an honest way, everybody gains something. Whereas, when they get up and share it in front of a hundred other adolescents, it's not that easy. In their embarrassment, they dumb down the experience. That's a place where myths have helped me.

HANSEN: Do you personally experience myth as psychoactive?

STALEY: When I was five years old, my ten-year-old brother was killed in a car accident. No one ever explained to me where he went, there was nothing. I mean, my parents were grieving, but no one ever came to this five-year-old and said, "You know, Joey is in heaven" or wherever—nothing. And so, that whole image of death has been something that I've had to deal with over and over again in my life. I was twenty-one when I was taking my Waldorf training, and this wonderful teacher told me the story of Gilgamesh. I was completely enthralled with it. It was going so deep in me. Gilgamesh is asking the question, "Do we all have to die?" It was so healing. I've loved that story ever since. The myth tells me that even though one-third of me is a human and two-thirds is God, I am still going to die. That's the place where that myth really spoke to me.

HANSEN: That's beautiful.

STALEY: It was wonderful. This isn't a myth, but Tolstoy's short story, "What Men Live By," also helped me with the issue of dying. It capped off Gilgamesh for me. In that story, this angel, Michael, was sent to Earth to learn what truths human beings live by. There's one scene where the angel Michael becomes a shoemaker, and a very wealthy man comes in, gives him the finest leather, and says, make me really good boots, but be careful, don't mess up here. But Michael doesn't make good boots, he

44

makes slippers and his master shoemaker is going crazy because this is the best leather. A little while later, the servant of the man comes back and says, "Our master's had an accident and needs the death slippers." One of the truths that Michael learns about human beings is that we don't know the time of our death. So, this story, as well as Gilgamesh, has helped me deal with the issue of death. The power of the story is very healing.

HANSEN: Stories can offer a kind of companionship. They give something deep inside of us a companion.

STALEY: Which is very different from expository writing, which says okay now, we don't have to be afraid of death. Everybody's going to die—ta-da, ta-da, ta-da. But when it's in a picture in a story, it has a completely different power.

I find that the theme of separation is particularly strong with high school students. What does it mean to have to separate, to go away? Another important theme is initiation and rites of passage. We explore the hero's rite of passage, and then I've had the students make up their own rite of passage. They are so wonderful. One girl's rite of passage was: *I would live in a glass bubble, and everybody would watch me. I would have to be silent and not answer back for two weeks. Then I would see the value of silence.* One boy imagined, *I'd be given a certain amount of money, and I'd have to go live in Hawaii, and I couldn't spend any other money. Then I would learn how to take care of myself.*

We talk in class about what the rites of passage are in America today. The answer is always the driver's license. Perhaps a student from a religious family might share about communion, or a bar or bat mitzvah. Without a clear rite of passage, how can you tell when you've gone from being a child to being a responsible person? This leads us into a discussion of markers in society to help youngsters recognize their changing roles. Michael Meade has written about this. What did it mean for a Native American boy to go off and spend two nights alone? We talk about vision quests. Some schools have a solo experience for their students. We recognize that adults can set up an event that might be a rite of passage, but they can't make it into a rite of passage. That is something that happens inside a person.

45

HANSEN: *(pause)* Let's talk about the pedagogy for a few minutes. You've given me quite a few examples of a dialogue process that you have with the class, and you've also spoken about going from the whole to the parts to the whole. I'd like to hear you talk about the role of art in teaching myth and then any other pedagogical tools or methods you'd like to discuss.

STALEY: One important skill is active listening. Students will read many stories, and then sometimes the teacher will just tell the story. When the students are listening to a story, they go right back into that early stage— you know, glazed eyes—I mean it's just fascinating—their eyes are sparkling —and they have a look of wonder. So, you need to have them be very receptive, to be good listeners. The next day we review the story. Pedagogically, it's being able to listen, it's being able to retell, and then it's being able to step into the story and find the patterns, find the main themes, the plot, and to extract it from the story and relate aspects of the story to life. A lot of listening and cognitive skills are being developed.

HANSEN: How do you facilitate that? All kids aren't necessarily brilliant listeners.

STALEY: I work to create a mood of intense listening. And it's practice, doing it over and over and over again. The Waldorf students have been doing this for years. We notice a big difference in the capacity of listening between longtime Waldorf students and new students transferring into the school. The new students often seem impatient with quiet listening, they seem uncomfortable with the silence. We speak about this. You have to really listen. If you're not listening well, then you're anticipating what will happen next. Then you're really only hearing yourself, your own thoughts.

You can also do listening exercises to heighten this capacity. You can do the exercise where they are sitting back to back. One person says something, the other repeats it to be sure the listening is accurate and adds something. It continues in this way. Students discover that concentrating on what someone else is saying can be tiring. And, sitting back to back can allow for an objective conversation, where the same topic could become uncomfortable if the two students were facing each other.

46

I think you need to build up respect for the oral tradition and how the oral tradition's been carried for thousands of years, mouth to ear, mouth to ear, mouth to ear from generation to generation. The bards would recite stories for hours and everybody would come to listen. The audience would learn the stories by heart. Oral tradition relied on rhythmic memory. We still have vestiges of this in nursery rhymes. Jack be nimble, Jack be quick. Jack jumps over the candlestick. Why do children remember these rhymes? Because of the rhythm. The old rope jumping games were based on rhythm. For example, Teddy Bear, Teddy Bear, turn around, round, round. Teddy Bear, Teddy Bear, touch the ground, ground, ground.

When you listen to a story, you find rhythm in the pattern. Papa Bear said the bed is too hard. Mama bear said the bed is too soft. Baby Bear said the bed is JUST RIGHT. Why is it so often that the third time is the right answer? You find that many children today have not been raised on fairy tales. They have not heard nursery rhymes. Their experience of rhythm is based on commercial jingles and rap music.

Another pedagogical skill is learning to comprehend the patterns. This is a cognitive skill. Most myths have such patterns, and the students begin to anticipate them, even when they hear the myth for the first time.

Then there are the writing skills involved in the study of myths. For example, I ask them to write a summary of a myth. They don't like this assignment because they want to relate the whole story back to me. The summary deadens the imagination, yet it is an important skill to develop. The students who are still in a younger state of consciousness want to hold on to the story itself. They want to narrate one scene after the other. Students who have become more objective find it easier to write a summary. These students have usually made a significant step into abstract thinking. They are able to summarize the key points of the story without relying on narrating the events.

Another writing assignment I use is to write a dialogue based on a scene from a myth. For example, write a scene where Gilgamesh and Enkidu are going off to kill the monster Humbaba. Write a dialogue, two pages, and make it true to character. Then we'll have them act their scenes out in class. So that's another pedagogical form. Poetry would be another writing skill. We would take a particular theme we've been working with and put it to poetry.

HANSEN: What about the role of art in teaching myth?

STALEY: We can work with a myth artistically in clay, drawing, or paint. The students are asked to come with an artistic exploration of either a myth or a theme from a myth. Another assignment is to have the students create their own myth. The teacher has to give clear directions and guidelines. Otherwise, many students will write in the style of science fiction with aliens and UFOs. The great myths that surround us today are connected with space. For example, *Star Wars*. I was told that *Star Wars* was conceived by three friends who were at USC together. They loved fairy tales and wanted to write a modern fairy tale. You can find so many archetypes in it.

HANSEN: Was George Lucas one of those three guys?

STALEY: I think so. And Gary Kurtz. Gary Kurtz's ex-wife was a neighbor of mine. Why does *Star Wars* capture the imagination of all ages? And *The Lord of the Rings* and *The Hobbit* also. Some of the kids will remember they loved the *Narnia* books when they were younger.

HANSEN: I think that the movie *The Matrix* is one of the new myths.

STALEY: Yes.

HANSEN: *Narnia* and *The Lord of the Rings* are pre-space age, pre-technology and are so different from our current life situation because of that.

STALEY: You want students to be able to see that myths are still alive. But I don't like to lose them into science fiction right away, because I think it cuts off many possibilities of imagination. We've got a myth going on right now. You know, we're the biggest, strongest, most powerful monster in the world. You could take the world situation right now and put it into a very interesting myth. I'm not sure what the ending is yet. When you're working with a class, again, with ninth grade you might have difficulty doing it, but by the time you got to eleventh or twelfth grades, if you put something out like that, there would be kids who would jump at that.

I just finished teaching *Moby Dick* up at the Rudolf Steiner College. We discussed who is Starbuck? He's the good man, he's loyal, he's thoughtful, he's trying to do anything he can to turn Ahab away from the whale. He even thinks about killing Ahab at one point, but he can't do it, he's so ethical. And the whole ship goes down. Scary. It just so happened that in the Sunday *Chronicle* there was a write-up, a parody of *Moby Dick* based on President George Bush. One of my adult students said, "Now I understand why we did it." She said, "Colin Powell is Starbuck."

HANSEN: Is George Ahab?

STALEY: Oh, I think so. Well, I'm not sure if Cheney is, or Bush is, or Wolfowitz—maybe Wolfowitz.

HANSEN: And Moby Dick?

STALEY: In this situation? Well, Bush is using Iraq as the Moby Dick, but he keeps heaping more things onto it, which is exactly what Ahab did. Ahab says, Moby Dick is all the evil that ever happened in the world. And you know, it's sort of like George Bush, Sr. saying this could be the "mother of all battles." It had to be this real David and Goliath issue, we had to make it big enough, then we put it into a myth. And we believe it. This would be the kind of really exciting conversation to have in the twelfth grade. Not to take a political position in the classroom, but just to look at what's going on. When twelfth graders understand the power of mythic images, they get excited about literature.

HANSEN: Wonderful!

STALEY: It's fun, isn't it?

HANSEN: You make it fun. You have already said quite a bit about which particular myths you use with adolescents, but I'm wondering if you want to say more.

STALEY: I think Demeter and Persephone are really important. Prometheus. It's almost unlimited with the Greeks; they're just so rich. The Amazons, the overthrow of the matriarchy, and the coming of the patriarchy. I also would introduce them to Riane Eisler's book *The Chalice and the Blade*. She speaks about Minoan myths—Minos, the labyrinth, Ariadne.

And the Norse myths—Waldorf students usually hear these in fourth grade, and then we would review them in the ninth grade. The Yggdrasil Tree, the Tree of Life, is in the Norse myths. Its roots go down in the lower worlds, the branches spreading, with the squirrel running up and down between the owl at the top and the snake at the bottom. An interesting image there. And then there is the well of Mimir. Odin loses his eye and gains inner vision. The Norse myths are very interesting from that point of view. The three Norns—past, present, and future—are represented by three women: one spins the thread, one measures the thread, and one cuts the thread. Here we have the picture of the span of life.

Other myths describe the Golden, Silver, Bronze, and Iron Ages showing that there's an ancient past, a loss of certain capacities, and gaining of new ones over time. Always this loss and gain. I think for the high school students it's really important to see that in everything we do, we lose something, we gain something.

Of course, Gilgamesh is important to use with adolescents. One that would fit in well with the study of India is Arjuna and Krishna, especially the discussion about giving up the garment of one life and gaining a new one the next time. This dialogue also speaks of the difference between killing indiscriminately and killing out of consciousness when one has to. This conversation between Arjuna and Krishna about killing is very important.

I've collected a lot of African myths, which I included in my book *Hear the Voice of the Griot.* The Yoruba tales and the Ashanti tales, which we tell in second grade, have a fable-like quality. Then there are the stories from the Old Testament. There are certain stories that we should be exposed to as part of our education: Abraham and Isaac, Jacob and Esau, and of course, Adam and Eve. One distinguishes these stories as literature rather than religion. I think one of the most important images is the picture of the two trees in the Garden of Eden: the Tree of Life and the Tree of the Knowledge of Good and Evil. As you know, God told Adam and Eve that they could eat as much as they wanted of the Tree of Life, but they could not eat of the Tree of Knowledge of Good and Evil. What happened when they ate the forbidden fruit? They became aware

50

that they were naked, they were ashamed and had to hide. Then they were driven out of Paradise, driven out onto the earth where they had to suffer. That's so powerful. From this time on, they have to deal with the burden of figuring out what is good and what is evil. Their innocence is lost. It takes you back to the image of Prometheus. Should he have left fire alone so that human beings would be dependent on the gods? Should Adam and Eve have stayed in the garden and not suffered? Where is our garden? What would it be like to be in a garden where you couldn't do anything wrong?

We can pick up this theme of freedom with *Brave New World* by Aldous Huxley. If you don't have choices, you can't make a mistake. You're drugged. You're always happy. Is that human? We continue that theme in twelfth grade with the Grand Inquisitor in the *Brothers Karamazov* by Dostoyevsky. Ivan is telling his story to his brother, Alyosha. The Grand Inquisitor says to Christ: *What you did was wrong. We had to change your message, because what you did was to give freedom to everyone. The strong people could handle it, but what about the weak people? We've taken away the pain from them so they can be happy. They can confess to us, and we will carry the burden.* This scene is so powerful. You see, it's all going to the same theme. In that situation, Christ believed—trusted—that human beings could handle freedom. We have some powerful conversations in twelfth grade about this: here's the same issue repeatedly in stories over time. People have been free. Have we solved all the problems? Was Christ wrong? Well, the Grand Inquisitor says He was. So, you start teaching myths and images at one age, and over the years you just keep spiraling around, coming back to the theme at a higher level.

HANSEN: It's fantastic what you're doing. That's a beautiful education.

CHAPTER THREE

Interview with
Kent Ferguson

Kent Ferguson is co-founder and Headmaster of the International School Down Under, located in New Zealand, where students age 16 through 19 study abroad for a semester. Prior to this, Ferguson co-founded another innovative grassroots private school, Santa Barbara Middle School, and served as its Headmaster from 1980 until 2000.

Kent Ferguson

Ferguson's educational vision weaves academics with mythology, rigorous outdoor learning adventures, athletics, and social service. His educational approach embraces hands-on experiences, community building within the school and with international partners, and authentic rites of passage.

Approximately twenty percent of Ferguson's adult life has been lived on the road, bicycling and traveling with students and educators, visiting every one of the fifty states and over thirty foreign countries. Ferguson has been affiliated with ten different educational institutions and has taught every grade from third through adult education.

MAREN HANSEN: When did you become the Headmaster at Santa Barbara Middle School? Was it in the autumn of 1980?

KENT FERGUSON: Yes.

HANSEN: And you were the headmaster until when?

FERGUSON: The end of 2000. I met in 1975 with the first Director, Margot Kenly, and others to share ideas and visions of what such a school might be and how it could make good use of Mother Nature and the natural environment. At that time, however, I was attempting to found my own "traveling school," the North American Odyssey. I came to the Santa Barbara Middle School in October of 1979 thinking that it would be a one year stopover on my way to an entirely mobile school. Margot wanted me to join the young faculty. We agreed that I would teach two days, a Thursday and a Friday, for free, so that she, the staff, and board members could observe these two classes. I remember the first day, a Thursday, I taught about Plato and Socrates, the Parthenon, and the teachers and the teachings of mythology. Friday I taught about the Hopi tradition. Those were my first two teaching experiences at the Santa Barbara Middle School. I shall never forget it!

HANSEN: I know that teaching myth to adolescents is something that's been important to you. What do you hope to achieve when you teach myth to adolescents?

FERGUSON: Maren, all of my life has been like a myth, and I have, since age fourteen, wanted to be an educator. The word "educator" means drawing out, drawing out something that's already in, in this case, in a human being. It's been my experience that nothing is as powerful and potent to do this as myth. For me personally, within my own life, I would say that's true. But also speaking as an educator, there is no doubt in my mind that the most profound educational experiences, the most charged atmosphere that I've ever seen classrooms—when electricity is in the air—has been in some way related to, and shaped by, evoking the presence of myth.

HANSEN: What do you think it is about myth that brings that profound experience?

INTERVIEW WITH KENT FERGUSON

FERGUSON: When I was a little tyke, I would do what your daughter is doing today. That is, I would tell my Mom that I was not feeling well and wanted to stay home from school. I'm saying that with a big smile as I suspect that your daughter now is rather like I was then: she's just half-happy to stay home, and half-ill. Well, I would do that, and as soon as I had convinced my mother that I didn't have to go to school—she was pretty easy to convince—bammo, I would be off to the neighbor's house getting out the old Bible stories. I was not then steeped in any religious tradition, but I loved these old stories; Joshua would do this, and Samson and Delilah would do that. When I wasn't reading the Bible stories, I would be reading those old comic books which Walt Disney and others were putting out. The ones that I read way back then—I'm sixty now— they were steeped in mythology. Mickey Mouse was re-enacting the Vikings in a child's cartoon, or going back to ancient Greece, or going back to old California. In truth, I learned to read and to enjoy reading by using the comics! I now realize that they gave me what I was hungry for: a larger vision of life, purpose, growth, adventure. I was seeking to make sense out of life, and very often school was not really of great help in that regard. My real education occurred out of school with these stories. There came a time when we got to study myth and story in school and the way they did it was bo-o-o-ring.

HANSEN: Wait, you were bored—?

FERGUSON: When I got to college and I started studying mythology.

HANSEN: The way they taught it was boring?

FERGUSON: Yes, that's right. Exactly. Because the way they taught it, they tried to make this academic thing out of it. We studied the story in pieces, a totally detached cognitive approach, to get a taste of a different culture, which we viewed as simple, uneducated, and certainly not our cultural equal. It was boring, and not connected in any real way to life. Later, after I was done with formal education as we know it, mythology came alive to me on many different levels. I loved the history in myths. Glorious history is actually a form of mythology. For example, the history of the ancient Greeks shaped Greek myths. The day that Dwight Johnson gave me the *Book of the Hopi* was a day that changed my life because that book, unlike all the other stuff that I'd read about anthropology, started with the myths, legends, and the world view of an ancient people, and it just rang true. And the door kept opening—into the Hindu myths, Mayan myths, Chinese myths, and now, in my sixties, I have found the stories of the ancient Waitaha people of New Zealand, where I now live.

There was one magical weekend in the 1980's in the nearby Ojai Valley, when I sat at the feet of Joseph Campbell. I feared at the beginning: *Oh, it's going to be boring, he's going to talk about the King Arthur stories, I don't like the King Arthur stories*, but he transformed me. As I sit here today at age sixty, I'm still identifying with knights and quests and swords. I mean, he transformed me. Together, this great teacher and I, and many others in the living room, entered Camelot and tasted it. Camelot raised us out of our lives, and yet at the same time put new meaning into our lives.

Then to read Alfred Lord Tennyson's *Idylls of the King* . . . .wow! Lord Tennyson remarked that as a boy he found King Arthur and all of that a bore. It was only when a dear friend of his died that, somehow, he began to see Arthur in his friend and his friend in Arthur. This can and does happen. That is important to understand: we can enter into myth and live it.

I, myself, was sort of living in this mythological world. I guess that, at my core, I still am. I was using mythological metaphors in my life, and that, then, permeated my teaching. I still remember teaching a group of sixth and seventh graders—probably this was thirty years ago—and they loved the class. One reason they loved the class was that although it was a history class, I would plug them into it. I would actually name one of the figures after one of them, you know, and they identified so strongly with the people in the story. They would go home and draw pictures of what they imagined, they would dream of it. I had hundreds of pictures up on the wall of the images that were coming out of these kids. I didn't understand the language then, but it was archetypal imagery. It just worked, Maren. That's the thing, it worked. It was not an educational theory. It was something that lit up a room. Kids saw it. Parents saw it. It was opening up minds and hearts.

HANSEN: Let's clarify what worked there. I want to understand what you did. It sounds like you took a myth, or you were saying, too, a story from history—

FERGUSON: Both.

HANSEN: And you encouraged the kids to establish a personal connection with that story by putting their names into the story. The story wasn't just something external to them.

FERGUSON: Yes, exactly. The college stuff was so boring because there was no place for you. What does this have to do with your own personal quest and your own search? When you see that that's you in the story, then all of a sudden you can't wait to see how the story ends. Or you think about how that person handled a situation, which is analogous to the situation you're now facing in life. How did Psyche do it? Or, how did the people come back together as a community after they had spread out into various tribes and groups? When it relates to life, then I want to know because it's real, it's a road map, it's a guideline to life realities. Later in my life, I came across teachers who were also reaching inside myth, such as Robert Johnson with his books *He, She,* and *We.* So were Robert Bly and others in the men's movement. But for me, it was all fresh, all new, something was unfolding out of life. And that is the way I wanted it to be for my own students as well. I still want that.

HANSEN: So one of the ways you did this was to put the names of your students into the story. That's a pretty big insinuation that this story is about you. Were there other things that you did to help the kids forge that personal connection to myth?

FERGUSON: Well, I tried to show that the story might be about you in some ways, but also you are much like the rest of humanity. Your life, your problems, and your challenges are not unique; others who began in your shoes—Cinderella, Arthur, Arjuna, Rama, Kokopelli—made something incredible out of being in those shoes.

Another thing comes to mind. I'll use myself as an example, and I'll bet there are many others like me. Why did Joseph Campbell ignite me? Because he was ignited. His teaching wasn't an academic dissertation. It was in a living room, and I sat on the floor at the feet of a teacher, and I could tell that Joseph Campbell felt that this is important stuff. This is a retired teacher—I don't know how old he was then—he was in his seventies, I guess, his health wasn't that great, he had to take a nap after lunch—and the myths were living in this man, they were coming through him. I could hear it in his voice. I could see it coming out of his heart. We were in another place. We were in another time. We weren't even in this century. We were gathered at the Round Table. We were part of something ancient, noble, true, enduring, and fragile.

So, what I'm trying to say here is that the teacher has to live and feel the myth. I think that in living a myth and acting like you're living it, (and not falsely, by the way), you enter into the story, and it's who you are. If someone was trying to figure out who you are, they'd say, "Well, sometimes he lives in this land of myth." That magnetizes an environment. It puts something in your words, in your emotions.

Another thing that worked for me with young people was to literally, physically, take them out of the classroom into a different landscape. Take them on an outer journey and an inner journey at the same time. Take them somewhere so that they can enter Camelot, enter ancient Athens, where they enter a magic grove, or where the kachinas come from. Let them put round stones on a piece of ground only to think of them as a medicine wheel, or a round table. For me, the most successful example of that, although there have been many, would be the American Four Corners, which provided me with a geography, a landscape, the remnants of an archeology, or an architecture—just enough hints as to what might have been. On top of that, then, we were able to receive the myths and legends of the Pueblo people. I found that the young people, essentially the white-skinned Americans, who have been most of my students, were as starved as I was. They were starved for this sort of thing. They were sometimes almost in rapture—seriously, some were—to be given certain imagery, certain keys within these stories.

Hansen: Can you flesh out an example of what you're talking about?

FERGUSON: There was a boy, Tim by name. I won't give a last name because he still lives here in our community. Tim was a shy boy who, in an academic setting, didn't have many successes going for him in the ways that our educational establishment considers success. He wasn't a good student, his report card was a disaster, he was clumsy, he did not have a sport at which he excelled, he was very quiet, and he was shy in class. He was on one of these trips I am mentioning. He hears these stories, and then there's this day of quiet—quiet time is essential to inner growth. Quietly and by himself, Tim clears an area about, say, ten feet by ten feet in the dirt. He's out in Arizona. He is sitting in the red clay. And he starts to build something with stones. In this case, it's the kiva of his imagination—how he saw it when he heard the story. Out of his imagination, a city, a community, a miniature town, begins to take shape. His inner wheels are spinning, creating out of stones. It was the kiva of this old story; it was round, it was the womb of Mother Earth, and in his mind's eye he could see people dancing in it, and he heard their stories and legends. This boy, who classroom teachers might describe as "needing to pay more attention" now crafted into his village many small items which were mentioned ever so fleetingly in the story, a story told in the dark in the cold, around a fire, the night before. Now, as Tim is quietly doing this, along come two or three other students, and they too quietly sit down in the dirt and continue to build this village. Twenty-four hours later, there is a sacred space in the middle of one hundred and some junior high kids running around to beat the band, but nobody would dream of stepping on this because it was made by them, it was magical, it's Tim's Village, it is the highest point of his young life so far. He has become the quiet leader of this whole thing; this whole thing was done in silence. Nobody said put the tree here, put the village there, put the kiva here, put the plaza there. No, it all came out of kind of a group consciousness. They were given a home out in the middle of nowhere—in the woods. There were outhouses, we didn't have running water, and these kids created something. If you were above it looking down you'd say, why it's the village where that story took place thousands of years ago! Why here's this, there's that, here are the trees, over there is where the boy and the girl met, you know.

Then, as years went by, I discovered another amazing thing: I would first tell the kids the stories, but then I'd also mention what Tim had done.

So Tim becomes part of a new mythology, part of the school. It's okay to be a quiet boy who gets dirty and wants to build with rocks because there's meaning in it and it's honored. So a mythology about a mythology starts to build, and the Santa Barbara Middle School has its own mythology about itself, you might say, its own heroes and questors, those that went before and honored the light. The saying or, if you will, mantra of the school becomes "Because of Them, Us." It means that because of the ancient ones, what they did and did not do, we are where we are now. Now the myth includes both those of thousands of years ago and the young twelve to fifteen-year-olds at this school who did something on this same trip a dozen years ago. The heroes and heroines emerge, both ancient and modern.

It was like being a chiropractor. You could see people's spines kind of *(sound of cracking)* like they were getting adjusted somehow by these stories. They were standing straighter. Some of the things that would come out of the mouths of young people at twelve or thirteen or fourteen! Your logical mind would say, "There's no possible way that this white-skinned lad from that background in Santa Barbara, California, at age thirteen could possibly be aware of the profundity of what he is now speaking about." You would ask yourself, "Where is this coming from?" because a few days before the trip this was the same local yokel who was trying to put the frog down the girl's blouse at recess. Some other entity was speaking here. Something was coming through the young people.

And so, living the myth yourself helps to convey the deep meanings. And, for me at least, it was valuable to take advantage of physical geography as well, what's in your neighborhood, you might say. But it is so, so important how you tell the story. I think there's great wisdom in the ancient Hindu caste system in which the storytellers were highly esteemed. Storytelling is your calling. This is what you do. Not everybody could tell the story, and I can see why. Let Hollywood tell the story of Helen of Troy or others, and you wish it had never been done, because it is a story told by people who have no idea what they are talking about and no idea what to emphasize. And then they're pumping this into the minds and hearts and psyches of young people. They have broken a thread that's been passed on for thousands of year just to make a buck. It makes me mad. I can understand why the Hopi and Zuni and Waitaha elders are fearful when their stories are written down by outsiders to be sold and studied in the classroom.

HANSEN: I notice that in your approach to teaching myth, honoring is important. You honor the story. And you chose to honor the boy who felt something and created something out of that Pueblo myth. You affirmed his living experience of the myth. That affirmation seems to me like an important teaching move that you made.

FERGUSON: When you want to do something with young people, you start with a few basics, and one of the most basic things is human respect. We all hope to receive it, and if you hope to receive it, try to give it. Just respect, just like human courtesy: listen to somebody, assume that they have a good heart. You don't have much evidence to the contrary, certainly not with young people. And who are you to say that they don't have powerful gifts? You would never want to say that they don't. They're here for a reason—if you are, they are. The whole goal of education, as I stated before, is to draw out. There is something in there. It's not your job as a teacher to pump it in; it's your job to allow it to come out. Then I think things almost fall into place. You set it up right, and you've increased the odds of success just with these few basic things.

HANSEN: Could you talk more about how you tell a story? I'm wondering if maybe you have a myth in mind that you teach to adolescents, and you could perhaps tell me some of the things you would emphasize in that story.

FERGUSON: Okay. Here's one story. I'm drawn to myth and story from all over the world. I wouldn't want to indicate that I think that the Southwestern people have a monopoly on myth, but I have used those myths frequently because geographically it was the closest source I could find. It was actually physically possible to go there and build the imagination of a school around it and use its architecture. In contrast would be myths about Shiva or Vishnu, equally powerful, but such a geographical distance that you can't actually gear up thirteen-year-olds to go there every year. So, with that in mind, here's one of the oft told stories in my career.

There is a young Navajo lad. Sometimes I've told this story about a girl. When it was told to me, it was a lad, and that's the way I'm going to tell it here today, to you. So there's a young lad, and it is time for him to go on a vision quest. This story would be told over several nights. Right away there are the questions of what is a vision quest and why go on one, and why go on one at this age. So all of these can be dealt with now or at the end as the youngster goes back and thinks about the story.

HANSEN: The whole story would not be told in one night?

FERGUSON: No, that's important, very important.

HANSEN: Tell me why.

FERGUSON: Some of the best stories have chapters. You know, you can only see this much on a Saturday morning, and now you have to stay tuned to what happens next Saturday. You enter into it. And things can change. There can be defeat grasped out of what looked like essential victory. There can be victory grasped out of essential defeat. It can be that you are at a total quagmire. How is anything sensible or good ever going to come out of where we are right now? Then people start to talk, or they don't, they are just in their minds, or they draw a picture about it. Now, if you can share the picture, or somebody tells what they see, others are being brought in by the picture, by the song. Now somebody's written a song about it. I saw that happen often. The story evokes a song. A girl, Amy, wrote a song, "Hands of Steel, Hands of Love." It's one of my favorite songs, no longer sung at the Middle School, but that came out of a story about what a good teacher is. And the kids understood it. Anyhow, back to the Navajo.

The boy is going on a vision quest. And he goes off to, let's say, the top of a mountain (it doesn't really matter where he is), and he realizes that he's supposed to be quiet, he's supposed to fast, and he is to enter into this adolescent land of magic. Well, now, that brings up a whole other day's worth of subjects, because there is such a thing as an adolescent form of magic. Yes, there is. Huge discussions can occur about that. One of my own beloved teachers, who himself came from India, used to tell us how important it was to fertilize the young person's imagination before the onset of sexual energy, otherwise the imagination would become captive to eros, at least until age nineteen, and perhaps forever.

So now in the story, this boy is out there on the mountain. He's fasting, he's throwing rocks, and he's carving stuff with his knife. He's allowed to have a knife. He's hungry as a horse. Not much is happening. Frankly, he's very bored. A good many days go by and, in fact, there are only three days left before he's supposed to go back to the village, and nothing has happened. This is a great disappointment because you're supposed to come back to the village to sit with the elders to tell them about your visions and your dreams, and then they give you a name and you're in adulthood. Your whole identity as an adult and your value in the village comes out of your vision quest, but his vision quest has been a total bust with three days left to go.

That night he goes to sleep and has this bizarre, weird dream. It is a nightmare. In the dream comes a big ogre, an ugly giant. This dumb brute shows up in the dream, and it's mocking him and it's pushing him, and it's challenging his manhood, telling him what little worth he is, dumb, skinny, and a weak, wimpy pushover. The brute is just shoving the kid, shoving the kid, shoving the kid, hitting him in the chest, pushing him back. The kid's up against the wall, doesn't know what to do. A fight ensues. He's fighting for every bit, he's fighting just to stay alive. It's every adolescent boy's nightmare. He's crying, he's screaming, he's fighting, and somehow in the morning he wakes up. He's sweating. He's just glad to be alive and hopes he never has a dream like that again.

Now, the next night... Back to sleep and the same ogre appears and the same scene is reenacted except what the young boy realizes is, *wow, this is almost a fifty-fifty fight. I'm still getting the bejeezus beat out of me, but I'm smarter than this brute, and I realize I can fake and I can dodge, and I can twist and move and I got a fighting chance—I have more confidence this time.*

Now, the final night of the vision quest arrives, and here the big ogre comes again. This time our lad is almost excited to see him come. He'd rather he didn't come, but he's not surprised that the ogre shows up. The boy thinks, *I'm ready for you and I've been thinking all day about the strategies and the moves, and each night I'm getting stronger and you're getting weaker.* This night they wrestle and they push and they yell, but this night our hero, shall we call him, picks up the brute. He actually, literally, has the brute in the form of an Egyptian Tao or a cross—and he let's out this incredible roar of triumph. He's actually picked up the giant, which is three times his size, and he starts doing a dance. He's spinning around looking at the stars with his mighty chant—*"I'm stronger than you"* and *"I hit you"* and *"I got you,"* but he loses his balance and falls. The ogre's head hits the ground, breaks his neck, and the ogre is dead. At first, our hero does a victory dance: "I won, I won, I won. I've defeated the ogre." Then all of a sudden, he slows down, and realizes: *wait, wait a minute now, that ogre could have broken my neck the first night within two minutes. That ogre could have pulverized me into mincemeat, into dust. That ogre let me pick him up. That ogre was not necessarily my worst enemy. That ogre brought out all kinds of wonderful things in me. That ogre, in fact—if there was anything to this vision quest idea at all that my elders have taught about for centuries— that ogre is the key to my lifelong identity and vision quest, and I'm supposed to go home with it, and I just killed it! What do I do now?* His heart is breaking, and he starts to cry. He's almost ashamed of himself: a thirteen-year-old boy with tears running down his cheeks, but that is the way he feels. *And what do I do now? What do I do now?*

Well, I'll give this brother/enemy/warrior/friend/teacher/dumb, stupid brute/physical body that I've just killed, I'll give it an honorable burial. Call it man's stuff, or warrior stuff, he deserves an honorable burial, and I'm going to give it to him. So he digs a hole in the ground, he puts the ogre in it, and he's crying all the time. He covers the body up, and he remembers to do chants. He burns some sage because he remembers that is done at funerals. He does the best he can. The next day it is time to go home.

He goes home like a beat puppy with his tail between his legs. He goes into the center of the village. The elders sit with him and he tells them his story. He's so embarrassed, he's so ashamed, he's so confused. They ask him what it means. He says, "I have no idea what it means."

They're not hard on him; they love him. He's surprised that they're not hard on him. They're not laughing at him, they're not chewing him out; they're listening and asking questions. He can't wait to get out of there. Finally, he gets out of there, and he's trying to get back to normal. One day he walks out of the village and not 500 yards from the village, he stops in amazement. *I can't believe it. Right here, right here, 500 yards from the village—this is where the fight took place! This is where it happened.* He can't get over this fact. This is just incredible to him. *What does this mean? This has got to mean something because the elders say that things that happen in one dimension can appear in another dimension, and what about the dreams, and . . . .*

He makes a vow. He will come back to this spot, just quietly. He will smooth out the ground, he will get on his knees like he did in his dream, and he will cry over his fallen friend that he didn't mean to kill. He meant to protect himself, but he didn't mean to kill the ogre, because the ogre let him pick him up and the ogre could have killed him, but didn't. There's no way that boy could have possibly picked up the ogre without the brute helping in the process. And so he weeps and he cries. He comes back again and again, he weeps and he cries, he gets on his knees and chants.

Now, three weeks go by—twenty-one days—three times seven. He gets down on his knees and cries. His tears sink into the soil and he notices that there's something growing. Something is coming up out of the soil, up out of the grave of the ogre. There's something growing up. Something has been recycled, reborn! He watches this thing grow. It gets bigger, bigger, bigger. It's straight and it just shoots up, reaching toward the sky. It gets about as tall as he is at age thirteen or fourteen, and it opens up, and right from its heart it gives the gift of a yellow cob of corn. But corn had never before been known. This is the ancient story of the gift of maize to humanity. This boy's wrestling, suffering, sacrifice; handling it right with the burial, the chants and the tears, has symbolically provided a sustaining gift. His journey brought the world's first cob of maize, which would feed his people! Out of a seemingly silly trip that turned into a tragic trip came one of the greatest gifts that the Navajo people have ever received: maize, corn, the corn mother.

You can see that after hearing that story somebody might say, "Well, maybe I'll pay a little more attention to a dream," or "Maybe a bad dream isn't always a bad dream," or "It's interesting to know that other people thought dreams were important," or "What's a vision quest?," or "What's the connection between tears and rain?," or "I'll treat food with a little more respect." It's hard to predict who will pick up on what.

The only request that I make as an educator is don't mock. Just don't mock. You don't have to understand what someone says; maybe it means nothing. That's a possibility. Maybe the whole story means nothing. Maybe the boy was hungry, or maybe he had indigestion and had some wild dreams. Or, maybe somebody just made up a lovely story that never really happened. That's all fair, but just don't mock. What I now believe as I approach sixty is that this approach of honoring, of respect, of gratitude, of "don't mock" opens doors. If one story is allowed in properly and welcomed, the others are on the way.

HANSEN: You told that story in the evening, around the campfire with the Santa Barbara Middle School, located temporarily in the Four Corners—

FERGUSON: —probably a hundred times.

HANSEN: Did you simply tell the story, or did you amplify it in any other ways?

FERGUSON: Uh, I would dance. At the time I didn't realize that's what I was doing. There is a certain theater quality to good teaching sometimes, so if in the story a young person is spinning around a big ogre, you as the storyteller can spin around extending your hands. If the boy in the story is frightened, you can cower. If the young boy in the story gets on his knees, you can get on your knees. If the young boy weeps, if you feel it, you can weep.

Hansen: You act the story out while you're telling it.

FERGUSON: Yes, but not falsely. Not like "Oh, now I have to generate tears." That's what I mean when I say you have to live it. You have to feel the archetypal quality. I mean, no, you didn't ever have a dream about corn, but you've had other dreams in your mind.

Alfred Lord Tennyson had a friend who died. When Tennyson encountered Arthur of the medieval legends, he realized, *well, Arthur was a lot like my friend. My friend had a lot of Arthur-like qualities. My friend was a noble king in our boyhood friendship that ended in our mid-twenties.* When Tennyson read about Arthur, he could see his friend in Arthur. So when he wrote *Idylls of the King*, he says, with tears, "I consecrate, I consecrate what I'm writing." I wept when I read it. You know, I consecrate to my friend. I consecrate to Arthur. I consecrate to the English-speaking people the idylls of the once and true, true king. It goes right up your spine.

When you tell these stories, including the one I've just told, the Navajo story, young people can see that you genuinely feel something in the story. My experience with young people has taught me something about teaching in general: show me a teacher who's passionate about anything, and the students will be enthusiastic. In fact, once I had a teacher who loved lacrosse, and inside of a year, half the kids in the school were walking around with lacrosse sticks! Young people are looking for somebody to identify with or something they like, something they believe in. In my own case, it was bicycles. In my youth I rode across the country and worked in a few bike shops. Heck, if you love bicycles, you can have a third of a school, an entire subgroup of kids get fascinated with bicycles. I have seen this again and again. It's just a gimmick, but they'll actually get excited about the wheels, the ball bearings, the chains, and the fact that each member of a school is like a spoke on a wheel, and that a wheel which is 'in true' is more effective than one that is not. A symbolic language can grow up around these physical truths, which can be enlarged into universal truths. Perhaps it doesn't matter where you begin. Just choose something you love, share it, encourage it, nurture it, and watch it flower!

This culture is so focused on being academic, which doesn't really mean anything in a deeper way, so far as I can tell. It doesn't relate to your psyche, it doesn't relate to your soul, it doesn't relate to who you are. Academics tend to be treated as isolated compartmentalized subjects, usually not integrated with what young people experience as important in their lives. Why go to school because it's got nothing to do with who you are, what you are, what you need, what you feel? But when you integrate academics with your personal psyche, lights go on.

So dance, kneel, cry. I am a horrible singer. I am tone deaf, actually. It's an embarrassment to listen to me sing. But there were times that I would sing while I was telling a story. I was almost humiliating myself because I was trying to honor the story so much. Why, a young person can see that and say, well, I'll do that too. If somebody's ready to try to honor these deeper things, I'm ready to try to honor them too. I think they also feel, if you expose yourself a little bit, I can expose myself. If you made an idiot out of yourself singing, well, tomorrow night I can make an idiot out of myself with a painting or a story or something that's, frankly, half-done and not too skilled, because you won't be able to laugh at me. I didn't laugh at you last night when you were on your knees singing like a frog. So it's safe. We can all make our best effort, and it's not as good as Hollywood would have it, but it's okay because we're out here in the dirt and the dark and it's just "I'd like to share something and it's safe to share it."

HANSEN: Do you refer to the story at any other time on the trip? Are the kids asked to do anything with the story, or is it brought up anywhere else?

FERGUSON: Yes. This is where some of the magic of teaching comes in. There are such things as teachable moments. This is one reason why I don't envy you your task of writing a mythological curriculum. In a certain way, I don't think a curriculum can be written. For example, the story I just told could be written down. But that doesn't mean the person who tells it feels it, understands it, or empathizes with it. We could say that now we'll have the kids spend an hour writing about it, but if the kids feel they have to write about it, then it's school again. Frankly, all you've done is taken something sacred and done what everybody does with sacred stuff. You know, now it's Tuesday and we'll have a quiz: How old was the boy? How many nights did they fight? Was the ogre 240 pounds or 270? How long was his hair? How many elders were in the circle? And, if you're not careful, you will have that young person dread the concept of another story being told because they already see how the game's rigged. You get a nice, vibrant story, a little song and dance, then you get seven hours worth of homework, and you get a C- because you couldn't even spell the word Navajo right on the quiz.

HANSEN: Tell me what you do.

FERGUSON: Well, let's see, a teachable moment. This is a little simplistic. A kid says, "Boy, I had a nightmare last night." You might say, "Oh, like the boy in the story." Now, that might work or might not work. You didn't formally give that youngster homework, but he might leave and begin to relate his nightmare to the story. Or he might review the nightmare, thinking "Maybe it wasn't a nightmare," or "Maybe there's something more in it." Or, "I think I understand more how that boy felt in the story." You can't predict. It's an open-ended assignment. The boy made an innocent statement. But you couldn't write it into a curriculum, you know, now make sure you say that on the Tuesday after the Friday that you told the story.

I used to teach the *Ramayana* in 9th grade. I had five classes, fifteen kids in a class. We only had five copies of the *Ramayana*, so each class had one copy. For example, Maren, you're up tomorrow, your name's on the board, tomorrow is your day, so here's the book and you're to read Chapter Three. Because there are so many things in your chapter, you might get lost, so you pick what you think are the three or four or five most important things in Chapter Thirteen to orally tell the class tomorrow. You only have three to five minutes—I'll time you—, and this is partly to protect you so that you have an excuse to sit down or to claim you knew more if only you had time. You can only use one three by five inch card with notes on it, three by five minutes, everything's three by five tomorrow. Now, you don't know where the book ends. This is Chapter Thirteen of seventy-five chapters. There's not a soul in the room that knows how this story ends. You're the only person in the room that's read Chapter Thirteen. Jesse's going to be doing Chapter Thirty-Five two weeks from now, and it's going to build, so don't get too lost on the fact that the demon had a red dress. But, on the other hand, if the story for two thousand years has said that the demon had a red dress and not a pink dress, maybe there's a reason why. So you have to try to figure out what are the three to five most important things in the story and then tell the class. Then the kids will ask you questions: "Well, I didn't understand, Maren, what about that demon? How do you see it?" Well, now, you might say, "I forgot to tell that because Kent said it had to be three things, but now that you're asking questions, I'll say it had a red dress."

Five different classes could be telling five different versions of the *Ramayana*. The names Rama and Sita will be in all five classes. They could take a quiz at the end—was the main character Rama? Was his wife's name so-and-so? But they've heard five different renditions of the *Ramayana*. What one class dwelled on, and got ignited about, and drew pictures about, and wrote songs about, maybe the third period class wouldn't even understand. They'd say, "What are you talking about? We're studying the *Ramayana* in our class." And you'd say, "Well, so are we, but this is the way we see it." So, these are living, teachable moments. There's a poem that's always meant a lot to me:

No spoken word
No written plea
Can tell young hearts
What men and women might be.
Not all the books on all the shelves,
But what the teachers are themselves.

That's why I don't think a curriculum can ever be written down. Ancient teachings can get ossified, myths can become trashed and thrashed and maybe even outgrow themselves. As I was telling my dear friend today, Brian McWilliams, who is a devoted teacher at Middle School, as much as I adore the Four Corners, I don't fight for it and die for it. It's not that we have to have kivas at the Middle School! The real truth is thrash the kiva if you want because it's not the kiva that's important, it's the spirit of it. If somebody wants to use legends from Alaska or from the Mayans, that's fine. The point is how it's done. Does it ignite the students? Do people link their lives into it? Hopi myths aren't better than other myths. Use the metaphors that ring true! For example, I wouldn't want the Middle School to say, "Oh that last story, the one about the Navajos, we have to make sure every year that it's built into the curriculum and it's told in March." You know, that's not right! You have to feel it. Maybe that story just doesn't fit this year. Just let it go. Move on. Next.

HANSEN: I'd like to hear what you think about the relationship between myth and human psychological development. Do you think they're related, and, if so, how?

FERGUSON: Okay, like the other questions, should I try to give the nickel answer, dime answer, quarter answer, or dollar answer? How big does it get? My own personal view is that much of what's called western psychology is dangerous, and it's dangerous because it actually attempts to define what a human being is. It is like the story of six blind men each telling the other what an elephant is, even though they've only touched part of the elephant in their investigations. Human psychology involves things which in our culture, in our time, might be referred to as more than human. They're more than physical, mental, intellectual, more than emotional. The power, one of the powers of myth and mythic imagery, is that it speaks to the totality of a human being. Mythology, in a sense, expands a view of psychology, and of the psyche, and of what it is to be a human. It lifts one out of one's current small circle. It places one in a larger context, of humanity, of the Earth, of time—but even a larger context within oneself. It places one to almost end where we began.

When I was teaching younger children, trying to make history come alive by telling a story, I would fit the kids into the story so Maren is Abraham Lincoln, or Mary Lincoln. But it just so happens that in the sixth grade, your best friend is Alice, who is now John Wilkes Booth. John Wilkes Booth had a perspective. Alice, who's John Wilkes Booth in our story, actually believes that (s)he's doing a good thing. You don't want Alice to be a clod—she's your best friend—so you're ready to listen to her talk about how (s)he actually believed (s)he was serving and helping people by killing you.

Well, what happens in your psyche—because your question is about the psyche and psychology—is that you realize that both Abraham Lincoln and John Wilkes Booth, or whoever else we put into this story, each has a perspective that you can link up to. I have a part of that in me.

There is another part of me that's Jesus. And there's another part of me that betrays him. There's another part of me that's the two other people on the cross. I'm using Christian images, you can go with this. But just choose any tradition; they live within your own psyche. Bring these figures into your psyche and it enlarges you, creates a balance—it creates a sense of tolerance.

I had a dear, dear teacher long since gone who used to make remarks that drove us all crazy, because they were too flippant. He once said, "Don't bother listening to any story or reading any book that hasn't been around for one hundred years." When you are age nineteen, you believe the only thing that's important is stuff that's been out in the last ten years, but he said don't even bother about it unless it's been around for one hundred years. So, of course we wanted to challenge this: *why would you ever make a statement like that? That's old-fashioned stuff. They didn't know about fashion bell-bottoms, they didn't have computers. I mean, they didn't know anything a hundred years ago! No jets, no telephones.* He replied, "If it's been around for one hundred years, it has spoken to at least four different generations, so there's something true in it. People who have computers find something true in that story, just like people who didn't have computers, so there's something larger in that story."

Well, here I am now toward the latter part of my life telling you that I think he was more right than wrong. At nineteen, I thought he was out to lunch. But now I see that if a several thousand year old Jewish story that came out of some place in a desert in the Middle East, a place that I've never lived in, rings true to me, a non-Jew in California, it speaks to the human psyche in a larger sense. There's something potent there.

Hansen: Is there anything else that you want to say before we conclude?

Ferguson: Only this. As I think about the future, I think what we've talked about today is one of the key ingredients, absolutely fundamental, that has to be brought back into education. That is why I honor your efforts to design a myth curriculum, even though I've said I think it's something that can't be written down. But, the idea of bringing myth back, enlivening and lighting it up, is so necessary. As you well know,

Joseph Campbell, when asked about the new mythology, said that the photographic image taken from outer space of this beautiful blue ball of earth would be the nucleus of the next mythology. I've thought about that for twenty years. In fact, I used to have that very picture hanging in my classroom. Just that very picture, just for the imagery; it's the idea again of the whole. I said earlier that western psychology doesn't deal with the whole. A child hearing about John Wilkes Booth and Lincoln can feel that they're both inside. This is more of a whole. The mythology of the future will deal with this more rounded whole.

I think it's a mistake to say, okay, now let's study Sumerian mythology, now let's study Indian mythology, now let's study New Zealand mythology, because the people who told those stories didn't tell them that way. They said, this is truth about the people. Now, of course, it so happens they thought they were *the* people. Now, we are the people, and the next great world teachers will, like all of them, be part of a mythology and add to it.

Thanks.